The Sainsbury Book of
CHEESE
Rhona Newman

CONTENTS

NOTES

Standard spoon measurements are used in all recipes
1 tablespoon = one 15 ml spoon
1 teaspoon = one 5 ml spoon
All spoon measures are level.

Fresh herbs are used unless otherwise stated. If
unobtainable substitute a bouquet garni of the
equivalent dried herbs, or use dried herbs instead but
halve the quantities stated.

Use freshly ground black pepper where pepper is
specified.

Ovens should be preheated to the specified temperature.

For all recipes, quantities are given in both metric and
imperial measures. Follow either set but not a mixture
of both, because they are not interchangeable.

Published exclusively for
J Sainsbury plc
Stamford Street, London SE1 9LL
by Cathay Books
59 Grosvenor Street, London W1

First Published 1982

© Cathay Books 1982
ISBN 0 86178 146 5

Printed in Hong Kong

INTRODUCTION

Cheese is a delicious way of preserving and concentrating milk nutrients. Today, hundreds of different cheeses are made all over the world. Some varieties are mass-produced in creameries, while others are still made on a small scale in local farmhouses. Many of the continental cheeses are now widely exported, giving us an endless variety to choose from.

Cheese is a highly nutritious food, containing more protein weight for weight than raw meat, fish or eggs. It is also an excellent source of calcium and contains useful amounts of vitamins A and D, making it an ideal food for children and vegetarians.

Above all, cheese is versatile. The recipes in this book use all sorts of cheeses to make tasty starters, main meals, cheesecakes and teabreads, as well as flans, pizzas and party snacks.

You will also find advice on serving cheeseboards for every occasion, plus information on storing, freezing and cooking with cheese. A country-by-country guide to the principal cheeses describes their appearance and flavour, and suggests the best way to enjoy them.

SERVING CHEESE

Cheese should be served at room temperature for optimum flavour, aroma and texture. Remove from the refrigerator 30 to 60 minutes before serving, depending on the temperature of the kitchen. This is most important with soft, matured cheeses such as Brie and Camembert. Do not allow them to become too warm, however, or they may deteriorate. Cream and curd cheeses should be served cool.

Presentation is important. A plain wooden board is the most traditional base to serve cheese on. Select cheeses and accompaniments according to the occasion.

For a simple lunch or supper two hard cheeses, one strong and one mild may be sufficient. A wider selection should include some soft cheeses – mild and matured. French bread and wholemeal rolls are ideal accompaniments for a snack meal, along with salad and fruit. Chutneys and pickles can also be served, but they should not be so strong that they mask the flavour of the cheese.

For an after–dinner cheeseboard, offer a wider selection of more unusual cheeses. Only a small wedge of each is required – trimmed of any dry or cracked pieces. Small cylindrical or roll cheeses can be left whole. Serve a selection of biscuits – some salted, some plain – and include semi-sweet biscuits for the softer cheeses. Water biscuits, wholemeal and bran biscuits go well with all cheeses.

Don't remove wrappings until the last moment to prevent the cheeses drying. Alternatively, arrange the cheeseboard and cover tightly with cling–film until required.

A garnish of parsley or tomato enhances the cheeseboard if the selection is fairly simple, but the more unusual cheeses are best left to speak for themselves. If only one or two cheeses are being served, a portion of grapes looks attractive with them. Serve additional fruit in a separate bowl.

STORING CHEESE

Keep all cheeses in a cool place or in the refrigerator, enclosed in a vacuum pack, cling film, foil or an airtight polythene container to prevent them from drying out.

Hard cheeses have good keeping qualities. If in good condition initially, they can be kept in a refrigerator for 2 to 4 weeks. Sometimes a mould may develop on the outside but this can be removed before eating the cheese.

Soft cheeses have a shorter shelf life, so should be used by the date suggested on the wrapper. Leave soft cheeses such as Brie and Camembert in their wrappings; keep them flat to prevent loss of shape and allow some air to circulate around the cheese. To ensure even maturing, it is a good idea to turn these cheeses every two days.

FREEZING CHEESE

As many cheeses keep well, it is rarely necessary to freeze them. It is possible to freeze hard, semi-hard, blue cheeses and matured soft cheeses, although changes in texture may occur; e.g. hard cheese may become more brittle. As a rule, the higher the fat content, the better the cheese will freeze.

Any cheese for freezing should be in prime condition and cut into 250 g (8 oz) pieces. Vacuum packs can be placed straight in the freezer; any other wrapping should be removed and the cheese re-wrapped in freezer cling-film or foil, then sealed in a polythene box or bag. Thaw cheeses in the refrigerator to allow the full flavour to return. Once frozen, some cheeses may be more susceptible to deterioration, and should therefore be used fairly quickly.

Small quantities of grated cheese in polythene bags in the freezer are useful for cooked dishes.

COOKING WITH CHEESE

Cheese enhances the flavour of many cooked dishes but it must be treated with care to avoid unpleasant changes in texture. It should always be heated slowly over a low heat, but especially for fondues and sauces.

If used as a topping to be browned under a grill, never place the dish under a fierce heat – this will make the cheese tough and stringy. Place under a medium heat just long enough to melt the cheese.

BRITISH CHEESES

These were named after the regions in which they were first made. They are now made in large creameries except for small quantities of Cheddar, Cheshire and Lancashire which are still made on farms.

1. Blue Stilton
2. Cheddar
3. Leicester
4. Windsor Red
5. Cheshire
6. Sage Derby
7. Wensleydale
8. Double Gloucester
9. Caerphilly
10. Lancashire
11. Sherwood with Pickle
12. Cotswold with Chives
13. Blue Cheshire

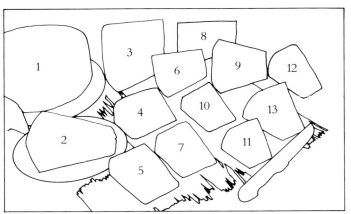

Cheddar is the most well known and famous English cheese, now imitated and produced in many other countries. It is a hard cheese with a close texture and varies in colour from pale straw to a golden orange. It has a full, nutty flavour varying in strength according to the time it is left to mature. Cheddar with the addition of chopped walnuts is also available.

Cheddar cheese is excellent used in cooked dishes, and is the traditional cheese served in a ploughman's lunch.

Farmhouse Cheddar is made in small quantities on farms. Traditionally it is made from the highest quality milk of the dairy herds. It has an excellent flavour.

Cheshire, the oldest British cheese, has a slightly crumbly texture and a mellow, slightly salty flavour. It is available white or orange, the latter being achieved with the addition of a vegetable dye.

Cheshire provides a good topping for grilling. It also makes an excellent accompaniment to semi-sweet biscuits and fruit.

Blue Cheshire is a deep golden-coloured cheese kept under special conditions to allow blue veining to develop. It has a rich, creamy, strong tangy flavour. This sought-after cheese should be reserved for the cheeseboard.

Double Gloucester is a hard cheese with a firm smooth texture. It is a golden orange colour and has a delicate creamy flavour. It is ideal for cooking or eating.

Cotswold with Chives is Double Gloucester cheese with the addition of chopped chives, which give it a distinctive flavour. It provides a good tangy flavour when used in cooking and is an interesting cheese to serve on the cheese-board.

Sherwood with Pickle is Double Gloucester cheese with the addition of pickle. A creamy, medium-flavoured cheese suitable for the cheeseboard.

Leicester is a rich russet-coloured cheese with a mild mellow flavour and open texture. It is good for cooking, particularly in Welsh Rarebit. Leicester has a tendency to dry out, so it should not be stored for too long.

Lancashire is a white, soft textured, crumbly cheese with a mild flavour. It is delicious on dishes to be browned under the grill and crumbled over soups and casseroles.

Caerphilly is a moist white cheese with a mild, slightly salty flavour and close texture. Its mildness makes it more suitable for eating than cooking. Good served with bread, celery, apples or other fruit.

Wensleydale is a mild, white cheese. It is close-textured, but crumbly, and has a slightly salty flavour. It goes well with fruit, especially apples – try it with apple pie.

Sage Derby is a close-textured Derby cheese, flavoured with chopped sage leaves – which give a characteristic green marbled effect. A distinctive flavour makes this an interesting cheese for cooking, or eating.

Blue Stilton – the 'king of cheeses'. Its distinctive blue veining is the result of a mould which is introduced into the cheese during manufacturing. Between the veining the cheese should be a rich creamy colour; a dry white cheese is a sign of immaturity. A mature stilton has a strong but subtle flavour, best appreciated when eaten with biscuits. Port is the traditional accompaniment.

White Stilton is a very white crumbly cheese, much milder than blue Stilton, but with a slightly sour flavour. It can be used for cooking or eating, and makes a good substitute for Greek Fetta cheese.

Windsor Red is Cheddar flavoured and marbled with red wine. It has a crumbly texture and a flavour similar to mild Cheddar; it is best appreciated when eaten with biscuits.

SOFT CHEESES

Curd Cheese is a medium-fat soft cheese with a maximum moisture content of 70 per cent and a mellow, slightly acid flavour. It is excellent used in cheesecakes, quiches, dips and spreads. Because of the high moisture content, curd cheese does not have a long shelf life and should be eaten soon after purchase.

Cottage Cheese is a low-fat curd cheese made from pasteurized skimmed milk – ideal for slimmers. It has a clean, mild flavour and a soft, granular texture – making it suitable for babies. Cottage cheese combines well with many foods, including salads, fruit, vegetables and biscuits; it is also used in cheesecakes. It should be eaten within a few days of purchase.

Cottage cheese is sold in cartons, plain or flavoured with chives, onion and pepper, pineapple, salmon and cucumber, Cheddar and onion.

Skimmed Milk Soft Cheese contains less than 1 per cent fat. It can be used as the basis for many dishes, sweet or savoury. Ideal for those trying to reduce calorie or fat intake.

Cream Cheese, sold in cartons, has a very high fat content. Its rich creamy flavour makes it ideal for spreading on bread or biscuits. Blend it with equal amounts of curd cheese for best results in cooked dishes.

A full-fat cream cheese is also available, in foil-wrapped blocks. This has a high fat content, but the processing makes it suitable to used in cooked dishes such as cheesecakes.

FRENCH CHEESES

It is possible to eat a different cheese every day in France as there are hundreds of varieties produced in this country.

1. Brie
2. Camembert
3. Coeurmandie
4. Caprice des Dieux
5. Neufchâtel
6. Bleu de Bresse
7. Chèvre
8. Fromage du Manet
9. Boursin
10. Tartare
11. St Julien (with garlic and parsley)
12. St Julien (with walnuts)
13. St Julien (with almonds)
14. Bleu d'Auvergne
15. Tomme au Raisin
16. Babybel
17. Roquefort
18. St Paulin
19. Port Salut
20. Petit Suisse

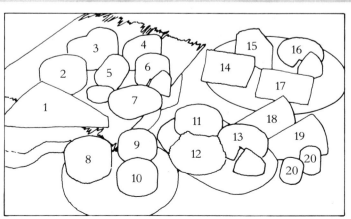

Only a relatively small number of French cheeses are imported into Britain, but these are becoming increasingly popular and better known, inspite of the immense variety of shapes and sizes.

Babybel is a smooth full-fat soft cheese with a red wax coating. It has a mild slightly sweet flavour, similar to Gouda. Babybel is small and disc-shaped, making it a good choice for the cheeseboard.

Bleu d'Auvergne is a blue cheese made primarily from cows' milk but including some goats' and ewes' milk. It is a rich cheese with a sharp salty taste – less delicate than Roquefort but similar in size and shape.

Bleu de Bresse is a small, dark blue veined cheese made from unskimmed cows' milk. It has a soft creamy texture with a thin grey-white rind and a rich piquant flavour. If allowed to become over-ripe, this cheese turns grey, dry and rather salty.

Boursin is a soft cream cheese made from enriched cows' milk. It is available flavoured with garlic, herbs or black pepper. It has a rich creamy flavour and is sold in small foil-wrapped packs. Boursin is delicious spread on savoury biscuits or crispbread.

Brie is one of the best known French cheeses. It is made from cows' milk in large rounds, about 35 cm (14 inches) in diameter and 7.5 cm (3 inches) thick. It has a white mould edible crust which encases a soft, pale cheese with a delicate creamy flavour.

Brie fermier is made on farms using modern methods and is considered better than the *Brie laitier* which is factory-made. Brie is ripe when the cheese has a consistent texture and bulges rather than runs from the crust. Any trace of an ammonia smell indicates that the cheese has turned sour. Brie flavoured with herbs is also available and makes an interesting alternative for the cheeseboard.

Camembert is made in creameries from the milk of the Normandy dairy herds. Prepared in small rounds, which are boxed or portioned and wrapped, it is a soft, creamy yellow cheese with an outer crust. Stronger than Brie, it should not be allowed to become over-ripe or it will taste bitter. When fully ripe the cheese should be soft and just bulge from the crust.

Caprice des Dieux is a small oval loaf-shaped cheese made with enriched cows' milk. It is similar in texture and flavour to Brie, but rather richer.

Chèvre is the generic name for goat's milk cheeses. Many varieties are made all over France, some with floury rinds and some with hard rinds. They are small and quite strong in flavour.

Coeurmandie is a small, heart-shaped creamy Camembert-type cheese with a velvety white rind. It is similar in flavour and texture to Brie, and is an attractive cheese to serve on the cheeseboard.

Fromage du Manet is a full-fat, soft cheese flavoured with garlic and herbs. An interesting cheese for the cheeseboard – ideal on cracker biscuits or crispbread.

Neufchâtel is a cows' milk cheese from Normandy. A soft, dark yellow cheese with a soft white coating and a slightly salty flavour. This cheese should not be allowed to become runny or discoloured if it is to be eaten at its best.

Petit Suisse is a soft cream cheese made from whole milk enriched with extra cream. It is unsalted and has a slightly sour flavour. To counteract this, it is often served with a little sugar. Petit suisse is sold in small cylindrical shapes, individually wrapped in foil. It is ideal for the cheeseboard and can also be used to thicken soups and sauces.

Port Salut is a semi-hard yellow cheese, which was first made by monks in the thirteenth century. Its bright orange rind encloses a smooth-textured, rather bland cheese; the flavour gets slightly stronger as the cheese ripens. It is almost identical to St Paulin.

Rambol Pepper is a processed cheese spread made from Emmental cheese and cream. It is flavoured with pepper and flamed with cognac. Beat eaten on biscuits.

Roquefort is a blue cheese made from ewes' milk curds sprinkled with breadcrumbs and specially treated with mould to give the characteristic blue-green veining. It is made in Aquitaine and is ripened in limestone caves, which provide the correct conditions for the cheese to develop its strong, rich, piquant flavour. At its best, Roquefort should be white with even veining. It is an excellent choice to end a meal. Roquefort is also used to make a delicious salad dressing.

St Julien is a full-fat processed cheese with a spreadable consistency. It is available in small rounds flavoured with garlic and parsley, hazelnuts, walnuts or almonds.

St Paulin is a semi-hard medium fat cheese with a bright orange rind. It has a mild flavour and is almost indistinguishable from Port Salut.

Tartare is a light, soft cream cheese flavoured with garlic and herbs, similar to Boursin.

Tomme au Raisin is an uncooked pressed cheese which does not mature with keeping. This smooth, slightly chewy cheese is coated with a mixture of dried black grape skins and pips, which add interest to its mild flavour.

ITALIAN CHEESES

The Italians export large quantities of their most famous cheeses and those listed below are becoming easier to obtain in this country.

Bel Paese is a popular Italian cheese with a firm white texture and a thin, dark yellow rind. It has a mild, delicate, slightly salty flavour. Bel Paese is usually served as a dessert cheese. It is also a good melting cheese, and is therefore useful in cooking, particularly as a substitute for Mozzarella. It keeps well if stored in a cool place.

Dolcelatte is a milder, creamier version of Gorgonzola. It is off-white in colour with blue-green veins running through it. To appreciate the flavour of this moist cheese, it is best eaten with biscuits.

Gorgonzola is one of the most famous cheeses throughout the world. It is named after the village of Gorgonzola near Milan, where is was originally made in caves over a thousand years ago. Gorgonzola is soft-textured and straw-coloured, with a characteristic blue-green veining. It has a rich, sharp, sometimes slightly spiced flavour. This cheese is at its best when firm and fairly dry.

Mozzarella is traditionally used for pizza toppings. It is a pale, smooth, close-textured cheese with a mild flavour. Bel Paese is the best substitute for Mozzarella.

Parmesan is the most famous Italian hard cheese. Made from skimmed cows' milk, it takes at least 2 years to mature and acquire its distinctive strong flavour. It has a fairly dry, flaky texture and is therefore excellent for grating. Because of its strong flavour, Parmesan is an excellent cooking cheese, and it is used, grated, on many Italian dishes, such as minestrone, pizzas and pasta. It is available by the piece or ready-grated, and although Parmesan is expensive, a little goes a long way to flavour any dish.

Dolcelatte; Bel Paese; Mozzarella; Gorgonzola; Parmesan

SWISS, GERMAN AND AUSTRIAN CHEESES

Emmental was originally a Swiss cheese, but it is now also produced in Denmark and Germany. It is a dull yellow cheese with holes 'or eyes' which should be evenly distributed. Emmental has a rather sweet, nutty flavour which makes it a suitable dessert cheese. It is also good for cooking, but it should not be heated too fiercely or it will draw threads and develop a stringy texture.

Gruyère is a hard Swiss cheese with a full, fruity flavour. It is a pale yellow cheese with fewer and smaller holes than Emmental and a hard brown rind. It is an excellent cooking cheese and is frequently used in quiches, cheese toppings and traditional Swiss fondues, often combined with Emmental. It is also good as an appetizer or dessert cheese.

Swiss Petit Gruyère is processed Gruyère cheese sold in boxed foil-wrapped triangles.

Bavarian Blue is a creamy, rich full-fat soft cheese with blue veining and a white mould surface. It has a tangy, creamy flavour and is milder than most blue-veined cheeses. A good choice for the cheeseboard.

Bavarian Soft Cheese is a full-fat, soft cream cheese, sometimes flavoured with horseradish. Both plain and flavoured varieties are good for spreading on biscuits, rye bread or wholemeal bread.

Bavarian Smoked is a cream-coloured processed cheese, smoked for added flavour. It is also available flavoured with small pieces of ham. It is made in large sausage shapes encased in a brown plastic skin and sold cut into thick slices and individually wrapped. A similar Austrian medium-fat smoked processed cheese is made in small sausage shapes, called 'Austrian links'.

Cambozola, also known as German Blue Brie, is a full-fat soft cheese with an edible mould crust, manufactured in a similar way to French Brie. It is a rich, creamy blue-veined cheese with a subtle flavour. Other imported German Brie cheeses are available – flavoured with herbs or black pepper.

The excellent flavour of these Bries makes them ideal for the cheeseboard.

Emmental; Cambozola; Bavarian Smoked Cheese; Austrian Links, Gruyère

DUTCH AND SCANDINAVIAN CHEESES

Edam, although named after the town of Edam in Holland, this cheese now has a trading centre in Alkmaar. It is a pale yellow ball-shaped cheese, weighing about 2 kg (4 lb), with a characteristic red wax rind. It is made from partially skimmed milk and has a lower fat content than most hard cheeses. It has a mild flavour and is used for cooking and eating.

Gouda is another famous Dutch cheese, made from whole cows' milk. Today most of it is factory-produced, but some is still made on farms from unpasteurized milk. It is richer, larger and yellower than Edam and has a characteristic dark yellow rind. This is rubbed with salt to help develop the flavour, which continues to improve for up to one year. It has a creamier and stronger flavour than Edam and is excellent in salads, sandwiches and cooked dishes.

Danish Blue also known as Danablu, is a milk-white cheese with a close pattern of blue-green veins. It has a rich creamy consistency and a strong tangy flavour. Good as a dessert cheese and as a snack with crispbreads or cracker biscuits.

Havarti is a Danish cheese made in rectangular loaf shapes or flat rounds. Pale yellow in colour with small irregularly distributed holes, it has an aromatic but mild flavour, partly due to the lack of a rind. After salting, the cheese is wrapped in transparent film and stored in this condition, which does not allow for surface ripening.

Jutland Blue is a Danish cheese with a high fat content and blue veins. It is more mature and therefore stronger than Danish blue cheese. Best reserved for eating.

Orange Roll is a Danish cream cheese, made from cream which has undergone various heat treatments. It is flavoured with Grand Marnier and orange, and coated with chopped hazelnuts. It has a mild creamy flavour and makes a rich addition to the cheeseboard.

Svenbo is a fairly new hard Danish cheese. It is made in flat rounds, or rectangular blocks, and has a dry yellow rind which may be coated with paraffin wax. The cheese has a firm texture with numerous holes irregularly dispersed throughout, and a characteristic, sweet flavour.

Jarlsberg is a hard cheese, revived in Norway this century. It is creamy yellow with large holes and a soft smooth texture. It is similar in flavour to Swiss Emmental, though milder and less aromatic.

Edam; Jarlsberg; Orange Roll; Svenbo; Havarti; Gouda; Danish Blue

SOUPS & STARTERS

Cheese is excellent for quick tasty soups and starters. Try hard-boiled eggs stuffed with any well-flavoured cheese, or a savoury cheese mould – flavoured with spices or freshly chopped herbs to taste. A mixed cheese pâté is a good way to use up slightly stale cheese. The starters in this chapter can also be served as part of a buffet.

Stilton and Cauliflower Soup

15 g (½ oz) butter
1 onion, chopped
1 cauliflower, broken
   into florets
600 ml (1 pint) light
   stock
1 bouquet garni
salt and pepper
1 tablespoon
   cornflour
300 ml (½ pint)
   milk
125 g (4 oz) blue
   Stilton, crumbled
chopped parsley to
   garnish

Melt the butter in a pan, add the onion and fry until soft. Add the cauliflower, stock, bouquet garni, and salt and pepper to taste. Bring to the boil, cover and simmer for 15 minutes; cool slightly. Remove the bouquet garni.

Sieve or work in an electric blender until smooth. Blend the cornflour with 2 tablespoons of the milk. Add to the purée with the remaining milk. Bring to the boil, stirring. Remove from the heat and stir in the cheese.

Pour into warmed individual soup bowls and garnish with parsley. Serve immediately.
Serves 4

Dutch Ham and Pea Soup

15 g (½ oz) butter
1 rasher streaky
   bacon, derinded
   and chopped
1 onion, chopped
600 ml (1 pint) light
   stock
500 g (1 lb) frozen
   peas
salt and pepper
grated nutmeg
sugar
1 tablespoon cornflour
300 ml (½ pint)
   milk
50 g (2 oz) ham,
   finely chopped
125 g (4 oz) Gouda
   cheese, grated
2 tablespoons single
   cream to garnish

Melt the butter in a pan, add the
bacon and onion and fry until soft.
Add the stock and bring to the boil.
Add the peas, bring back to the boil,
cover and simmer for 15 minutes.
Cool slightly, then sieve or work in
an electric blender until smooth.

Return to the pan and add salt,
pepper, nutmeg and sugar to taste.
Blend the cornflour with
2 tablespoons of the milk. Add to
the soup with the remaining milk
and heat, stirring, until the soup
thickens. Stir in the ham and 75 g
(3 oz) of the cheese. Heat through
gently and check the seasoning.

Pour into warmed individual soup
bowls. Swirl a little cream into each
and sprinkle with the remaining
cheese. Serve immediately.

Serves 4

Cheesy Chowder

50 g (2 oz) streaky
  bacon, derinded
1 large onion
1 celery stick
250 g (8 oz) potato
15 g (½ oz) butter
450 ml (¾ pint)
  light stock
1 bay leaf
salt and pepper
grated nutmeg
450 ml (¾ pint)
  milk
1 × 198 g (7 oz)
  can sweetcorn,
  drained
50 g (2 oz) peeled
  prawns
75 g (3 oz) Cheddar
  cheese, grated
chopped parsley to
  garnish

Chop the bacon, onion, celery and potato. Melt the butter in a large pan, add the bacon and onion and fry until soft. Add the celery, potato, stock, bay leaf, and salt, pepper and nutmeg to taste. Bring to the boil, cover and simmer for 20 minutes or until the potato is cooked.

Stir in the milk, sweetcorn and prawns. Heat through gently and check the seasoning. Pour into warmed individual soup bowls and sprinkle with the cheese and parsley.

Serves 4 to 6

NOTE: This is a substantial soup which can be served with crusty rolls as a light meal.

Cheese and Prawn Cocktail

few lettuce leaves
125 g (4 oz)
    Caerphilly cheese,
    diced
50 g (2 oz) peeled
    prawns
2 celery sticks,
    chopped
5 cm (2 inch) piece
    of cucumber,
    diced
DRESSING:
2 tablespoons salad
    cream
2 tablespoons tomato
    ketchup
1 tablespoon low-fat
    natural yogurt
salt and pepper
TO GARNISH:
4 cooked whole
    prawns (optional)

Shred the lettuce and divide between 4 individual glass dishes. Mix together the cheese, prawns, celery and cucumber, then divide between the glasses.

For the dressing, blend the salad cream, tomato ketchup and yogurt together. Add salt and pepper to taste.

Just before serving, spoon the dressing over the cocktails and garnish each one with a whole prawn, if liked.
Serves 4

Savoury Cheese Mould

227 g (8 oz)
  medium-fat curd
  cheese
2 teaspoons finely
  chopped onion
2 tomatoes, skinned,
  seeded and finely
  chopped
1 tablespoon anchovy
  fish paste
few drops of anchovy
  essence
salt and pepper
TO GARNISH:
shredded lettuce
parsley sprigs
tomato slices

Place the curd cheese in a bowl and
add the onion, tomatoes, anchovy
paste and essence. Blend well and
add salt and pepper to taste. Press
into an oiled 300 ml (½ pint) mould
or the cheese carton. Chill in the
refrigerator for 2 to 3 hours.

Turn out onto a serving dish and
surround with lettuce. Garnish with
parsley and tomato. Serve with rye
bread, toast or crispbreads.

Serves 4

VARIATIONS:

1. Omit the tomatoes, anchovy paste
and essence and add 1 teaspoon made
mustard and 25 g (1 oz) finely
chopped walnuts.

2. Replace the anchovy paste and
essence with 2 teaspoons each
chopped parsley, chives and thyme.

Mixed Cheese Pâté

*75 g (3 oz) Danish
  blue vein cheese*
*50 g (2 oz)
  Wensleydale
  cheese, grated*
*50 g (2 oz) Double
  Gloucester cheese,
  grated*
*2 tablespoons natural
  low-fat yogurt*
*4 tablespoons single
  cream*
*2 teaspoons chopped
  chives*
*2 teaspoons chopped
  parsley*
*¼ teaspoon made
  mustard*
*parsley sprigs to
  garnish*

Mash the Danish blue cheese until soft, then add the Wensleydale and Double Gloucester. Mix together with the yogurt and cream. Add the chives, parsley and mustard and mix until well blended.

Transfer to a serving bowl and chill overnight. Remove from the refrigerator 1 hour before serving and garnish with parsley.

Serve with rye bread, melba toast or crispbreads.

Serves 4 to 6

NOTE: This piquant cheese pâté is delicious served as a savoury to round off a meal.

Leicester Kipper Pâté

250 g (8 oz) kipper
    fillets, skin
    removed
1 tablespoon lemon
    juice
4 tablespoons milk
4 tablespoons natural
    low-fat yogurt
75 g (3 oz) Leicester
    cheese, grated
pepper
TO GARNISH:
parsley sprigs
lemon slices

Poach the kippers in the lemon juice and milk for 10 minutes. Drain, reserving the liquor. Place the fish in a bowl and mash until smooth. Blend in the yogurt, cheese and sufficient liquor to give a smooth consistency. Add pepper to taste and spoon into 4 small dishes. Chill until required.

Garnish with parsley and lemon slices and serve with melba toast.

Serves 4

Sardine Fish Cream

113 g (4 oz)
    medium-fat curd
    cheese
1 × 120 g (4¼ oz)
    can sardines in
    tomato
2 teaspoons chopped
    chives
2 spring onions,
    finely chopped
3 drops
    Worcestershire
    sauce
1 teaspoon lemon
    juice
salt and pepper
chopped chives to
    garnish

Place the cheese and sardines with their juice in a bowl and mash together. Add the chives, spring onions, Worcestershire sauce, lemon juice, and salt and pepper to taste. Mix well.

Spoon the sardine mixture into a small serving bowl and garnish with chives. Serve with wholemeal bread or crispbread.

Serves 4

Boursin-Stuffed Eggs

4 hard-boiled eggs
50 g (2 oz) Boursin
   cheese with garlic
3 tablespoons single
   cream
15 g (½ oz)
   walnuts, finely
   chopped
salt and pepper
½ lettuce, shredded
paprika to garnish

Cut the eggs in half lengthways and remove the yolks. Place in a bowl with the Boursin and cream and blend well. Add the walnuts, and salt and pepper to taste. Spoon or pipe the mixture into the egg white halves.

Arrange the lettuce on a serving plate, place the eggs on top and sprinkle with paprika. Serve with brown bread and butter.

Serves 4

FONDUES, CHEESE & WINE, BUFFET PARTIES

A cheese fondue is a good way to entertain informally. Made in a special fondue pan or heavy-based flameproof pan, the mixture is first heated on a cooker then kept warm at the table over a spirit burner. It is traditionally served with cubes of bread, though sometimes raw vegetables, cooked meat or fish are served. These foods are speared onto long-handled forks and dipped into the fondue. One fondue will serve 4 to 6; one or more can be served as part of a buffet.

Cheese and wine parties are also an excellent way to entertain informally. The basic guidelines for cheeseboards apply (see page 6), but as there will be more guests than at a dinner party, have several cheeseboards and a wide selection of cheeses, including hard, soft, strong, mild and blue-veined. Overall there should be a good selection of flavours, textures and colours. For large gatherings it's a good idea to cut

the hard cheeses into cubes and pile them onto dishes; other cheeses can be cut into wedges or left whole. Allow about 75 g (3 oz) per person.

The accompaniments should complement the cheese and enhance the display. Offer a selection of different breads, including French sticks, wholemeal bread, rye bread and crispbreads, and, of course, biscuits. A small selection of mild pickles is appropriate. Crisp salad vegetables are also a good accompaniment, especially celery, tomato, radishes, cucumber, carrot and cauliflower. Make sure you have enough butter dishes around the table, allowing approximately 250 g (8 oz) for every 15 to 20 guests.

Fruits look attractive on the table and can be eaten with the cheese, or afterwards. Apples, grapes, pineapple and small oranges are particularly good.

If you want to extend your basic cheese and wine party and offer a selection of savoury party snacks, choose from the recipes in this chapter and reduce the amount of cheese served to 25–50 g (1–2 oz) per person.

Buffet parties are ideal when catering for larger numbers. Most recipes in this chapter are suitable for a finger buffet. If giving a light buffet for 30 people, serve about eight of these recipes plus a cheeseboard and accompaniments. Alternatively make 4 or 5 recipes and double the quantities.

Sample Buffet for 30 Guests

West Country Fondue
Barbecue Dip
Savoury Straws
Cheese and Apricot Whirls
Savoury Cheese Horns
Garlic Sausage Spears
Cheese and Nut Cubes
Cheese and Orange Eclairs

Cheeseboard
2 jugs of celery
1 bowl of cucumber chunks
2 bowls of tomato pieces
1 bowl of radishes
chutneys
selection of crisps, nuts,
breads and savoury biscuits

West Country Fondue

½ small onion, cut
300 ml (½ pint) dry
  cider
1 teaspoon lemon
  juice
500 g (1 lb) Farm-
  house Cheddar
  cheese, grated
1 tablespoon cornflour
2 tablespoons sherry
pinch of dry mustard
1 teaspoon Worcester-
  shire sauce
pepper
French bread cubes to
  serve

Rub the inside of a flameproof dish
with the cut side of the onion. Add
the cider and lemon juice and heat
until bubbling. Gradually stir in the
cheese and heat gently, stirring, until
it melts and begins to cook.

Blend the cornflour with the
sherry and add the mustard,
Worcestershire sauce and pepper to
taste. Add to the cheese and continue
to heat, stirring, for 2 to 3 minutes
until the mixture is thick and
creamy.

Serve immediately, with the bread
cubes.

Serves 6

Swiss Cheese Fondue

1 clove garlic, cut
150 ml (¼ pint) dry
  white wine
1 teaspoon lemon
  juice
175 g (6 oz) Gruyère
  cheese, grated
175 g (6 oz)
  Emmental cheese,
  grated
1 teaspoon cornflour
2 tablespoons kirsch
pepper
grated nutmeg
French bread cubes to
  serve

Rub the inside of a flameproof dish
with the cut garlic. Pour in the wine
and lemon juice and heat gently until
bubbling. Gradually stir in the cheeses
and heat slowly, stirring, until the
cheese melts and begins to cook.

Blend the cornflour with the
kirsch. Add to the cheese and
continue to cook for 2 to 3 minutes,
stirring, until the mixture is thick
and creamy. Add pepper and nutmeg
to taste.

Serve immediately, with the bread
cubes.

Serves 4 to 6
Illustrated on page 34.

Anchovy and Prawn Fondue

1 clove garlic, cut
150 ml (¼ pint) dry
    white wine
125 g (4 oz) Gruyère
    cheese, grated
250 g (8 oz) Cheddar
    cheese, grated
1 teaspoon cornflour
2 tablespoons dry
    sherry
2 teaspoons anchovy
    essence
Tabasco sauce
cayenne pepper
TO SERVE:
125 g (4 oz) peeled
    prawns
French bread cubes or
    toast squares

Rub the inside of a flameproof dish with the cut garlic and pour in the wine. Heat gently until bubbling, then gradually stir in the cheeses. Heat gently, stirring, until the cheese melts and begins to cook.

Blend the cornflour with the sherry and add the anchovy essence, Tabasco and cayenne to taste. Stir into the cheese and heat gently, stirring, for 2 to 3 minutes, until the mixture is thick and creamy.

Serve immediately, with the prawns and bread cubes or toast.
Serves 4 to 6

Avocado and Cheese Fondue

2 avocados
2 tablespoons lemon
    juice
15 g (½ oz) butter
1 clove garlic, crushed
1 onion, finely
    chopped
150 ml (¼ pint) dry
    cider
175 g (6 oz)
    Lancashire cheese,
    crumbled
2 teaspoons cornflour
4 tablespoons single
    cream
salt and pepper
TO SERVE:
French bread cubes
selection of raw
    vegetables, cut into
    strips

Peel the avocados, halve and remove the stones. Sprinkle with the lemon juice and mash the avocado flesh, or purée in an electric blender.

Melt the butter in a flameproof dish, add the garlic and onion and fry until soft but not brown. Add the cider and heat until just bubbling, then gradually stir in the cheese. Continue to heat gently until the cheese melts and begins to cook.

Blend the cornflour with the cream and add to the cheese with the avocado purée, and salt and pepper to taste. Heat gently, stirring, for 2 to 3 minutes.

Serve hot, or cold as a dip, with the bread and vegetables.
Serves 4 to 6

Anchovy and Prawn Fondue; Swiss Cheese Fondue; Avocado and Cheese Fondue

Open Sandwiches

These are ideal for small buffet parties. Use any of the suggested bases, spread with butter. Place a slice of one of the cheeses on top. Select a topping and one or more of the garnishes to complement the cheese in flavour, but provide contrast in colour. Arrange the open sandwiches on plates.

Bases:
white bread
brown bread
French bread
rye bread
crispbreads

Toppings:
sliced cold meats
salami
pâté
chicken
sardines
prawns

Cheeses:
Cheddar
Leicester
Double Gloucester
Edam
Gouda
Emmental
Gruyère
Jarlsberg
Danish blue vein
Blue Stilton
Cottage cheese
Cream cheese

Garnishes:
onion rings
parsley
cucumber twists
watercress
tomatoes
gherkin fans
olives
hard–boiled eggs
red pepper slices
shredded lettuce
grapes
pineapple
orange slices

Savoury Straws

125 g (4 oz) plain
  flour
pinch of salt
pinch of cayenne
  pepper
50 g (2 oz)
  margarine
50 g (2 oz) matured
  Cheddar cheese,
  grated
1 egg yolk
2 teaspoons tomato
  ketchup
2-3 teaspoons water
beaten egg to glaze
paprika

Sift the flour, salt and cayenne into a
bowl. Rub in the margarine until the
mixture resembles breadcrumbs. Stir
in the cheese. Add the egg yolk,
ketchup and enough water to make a
stiff dough.

Turn onto a floured surface and
roll out to a rectangle 5 mm (¼ inch)
thick. Brush with the egg and
sprinkle with paprika. Cut into
strips, then cut again to make straws
7.5 cm (3 inches) long. Place on a
greased baking sheet and bake in a
preheated moderately hot oven,
200°C (400°F), Gas Mark 6, for 10 to
15 minutes until pale golden. Cool
on a wire rack.

Arrange the straws on a plate or
stand in small pots to serve.

Makes about 50

VARIATION: Cut the pastry into small
biscuit rounds with a 4 cm (1½ inch)
plain cutter. Cook as above. Top
with curd or cream cheese and
sprinkle with poppy seeds to serve.

Cheese and Apricot Whirls

113 g (4 oz) cream
  cheese
3 tablespoons milk
50 g (2 oz) matured
  Cheddar cheese,
  finely grated
salt and pepper
1 × 411 g (14½ oz)
  can apricot halves,
  drained thoroughly
TO GARNISH:
paprika
walnut pieces
shredded lettuce

Place the cream cheese in a bowl and beat with a wooden spoon to soften. Blend in the milk and Cheddar, then add salt and pepper to taste.

Place the mixture in a piping bag fitted with a 1 cm (½ inch) star nozzle and pipe a whirl of filling into each apricot half. Sprinkle with paprika and top with walnut pieces.

Arrange the lettuce on a serving plate and place the apricots on top.

Makes about 10

NOTE: Any remaining cheese mixture can be piped onto savoury biscuits.

Crispy Sausage Balls

350 g (12 oz) pork
  sausage meat
125 g (4 oz)
  matured Cheddar
  cheese, grated
75 g (3 oz) rolled
  oats
½ teaspoon chopped
  mixed herbs
1 clove garlic, crushed
salt and pepper
1 egg, beaten

Place the sausage meat, cheese, oats, herbs, garlic, and salt and pepper to taste in a bowl. Mix well and bind together with the egg.

On a floured surface, shape into 16 balls. Place on a baking sheet and bake in a preheated moderately hot oven, 190°C (375°F), Gas Mark 5, for 30 minutes. Serve hot or cold, with Barbecue dip (see page 40) or a homemade tomato sauce.

Makes 16

Mini Pancake Kebabs

PANCAKES:
125 g (4 oz) plain
  flour
pinch of salt
1 egg
300 ml (½ pint)
  milk
oil for frying
FILLING:
250 g (8 oz) Cheddar
  with walnuts
3 ham slices
TO GARNISH:
grated cheese

Make the pancakes as for Seafood pancakes (see page 60), using 1 tablespoon batter for each one. Cut the cheese and ham into strips.

Place a piece of cheese and ham on each pancake. Roll up and sprinkle with a little grated cheese. Place under a preheated moderate grill until bubbling. Secure with cocktail sticks and serve hot.

Makes 24

VARIATIONS: Omit the ham. Use blue Stilton or sage Derby instead of the Cheddar.

Barbecue Dip

3 spring onions
½ green pepper
125 g (4 oz) red
   Cheddar cheese
150 g (5 oz) natural
   low-fat yogurt
1 tablespoon tomato
   ketchup
1 tablespoon
   mayonnaise
½ teaspoon
   Worcestershire
   sauce
Tabasco sauce
salt and pepper
TO GARNISH:
paprika or chopped
   chives

Finely chop the spring onions and green pepper, discarding the core and seeds. Grate the cheese, using a fine grater.

Combine all of the dip ingredients in a bowl adding Tabasco, salt and pepper to taste; mix well. Spoon into a serving dish and chill.

Sprinkle with paprika or chives. Serve with a selection of savoury biscuits and raw vegetables, such as red and green pepper, carrot, celery, cucumber and cauliflower florets.
Serves 6 to 8

Fruity Cheese Dip

227 g (8 oz) cottage
    cheese with
    pineapple
50 g (2 oz) Leicester
    cheese, finely
    grated
4 tablespoons double
    cream, whipped
finely grated rind of
    1 orange
8 green grapes, seeded
    and chopped
1 celery stick,
    chopped
celery salt
salt and pepper
parsley sprig to
    garnish

Place the cheeses and cream in a
bowl and mix well. Stir in the
orange rind, grapes and celery. Add
celery salt, salt and pepper to taste.
Pile into a serving bowl and chill.

Garnish with parsley and serve
with a selection of the following:
crisps, savoury biscuits, cubes of
French bread, Melba toast, raw
carrot, celery, cucumber, cauliflower
florets, radishes.

Serves 6 to 8

Savoury Cheese Horns

1 × 368 g (13 oz)
  packet frozen puff
  pastry, thawed
beaten egg to glaze
FILLING:
150 ml (¼ pint)
  double cream,
  whipped
125 g (4 oz) red
  Cheshire cheese,
  finely grated
50 g (2 oz) blue
  Cheshire cheese,
  finely grated
pinch of cayenne
  pepper
pinch of dry mustard
1 tablespoon chopped
  parsley
salt and pepper
TO GARNISH:
parsley sprigs

Roll out the pastry into a rectangle, about 25 × 30 cm (10 × 12 inches), and trim the edges. Cut into 12 strips, about 2.5 cm (1 inch) wide. Dampen one long edge of each strip and wind around 12 greased horn cases, starting at the pointed end, and overlapping by about 5 mm (¼ inch). Gently press the edges together.

Place on a dampened baking sheet and brush with beaten egg. Bake in a preheated hot oven, 230°C (450°F), Gas Mark 8, for 10 to 15 minutes. Remove from the cases and return to the oven for 5 minutes. Cool on a wire rack.

Meanwhile, make the filling. Combine the cream, cheeses, cayenne, mustard, parsley, and salt and pepper to taste.

Spoon or pipe the mixture into the horn cases and garnish with parsley sprigs to serve.
Makes 12

Cheese and Orange Eclairs

CHOUX PASTRY:
150 ml (¼ pint)
  water
50 g (2 oz) butter
65 g (2½ oz) plain
  flour, sifted
salt and pepper
2 eggs, beaten
50 g (2 oz) Cheddar
  cheese, grated
FILLING:
75 g (3 oz) medium-
  fat curd cheese
75 g (3 oz) matured
  Cheddar cheese,
  finely grated
finely grated rind of
  1 orange
1 × 212 g (11 oz)
  can mandarin
  oranges, drained
  and chopped
6 tablespoons double
  cream, whipped
TO GARNISH:
orange slices

Make the choux pastry as for Tuna Gougère (see page 59).

Spoon the mixture into a piping bag, fitted with a 1 cm (½ inch) plain nozzle, and pipe 5 cm (2 inch) lengths, or small mounds onto greased baking sheets, spacing them well apart.

Bake in a preheated moderately hot oven, 200°C (400°F), Gas Mark 6, for 20 minutes, or until well risen and golden brown. Make a slit in the side of each éclair to allow the steam to escape. Transfer to a wire rack to cool.

Meanwhile, make the filling. Place the curd cheese in a bowl and blend in the Cheddar, orange rind and mandarin oranges. Fold in the cream.

Fill the éclairs with the cheese mixture and arrange on a serving plate. Garnish with orange slices.
Makes 18
NOTE: When fresh mandarin oranges are in season, use these in place of canned ones.

Cheese Kebabs

250 g (8 oz)
  chipolata sausages
1 × 227 g (8 oz)
  can pineapple
  slices
1/4 cucumber, cubed
6 tomatoes, quartered
250 g (8 oz) Cheddar
  cheese, cubed
12 stoned dates,
  halved
1 grapefruit

Grill the chipolatas, turning frequently, until cooked. Cool and cut into 2.5 cm (1 inch) pieces.

Drain and chop the pineapple. Thread pieces of sausage, pineapple, cucumber, tomato, cheese and date onto cocktail sticks.

Cut a slice from the grapefruit to enable it to stand, cut side down. Stick the small kebabs into the grapefruit.
Makes 24

Cheese and Nut Cubes

227 g (8 oz) cottage
  cheese with onion
  and pepper
75 g (3 oz) Double
  Gloucester cheese,
  finely grated
75 g (3 oz)
  Wensleydale cheese,
  finely grated
3 tablespoons
  asparagus soup
  mix
3 spring onions,
  finely chopped
Tabasco sauce
75 g (3 oz) salted
  peanuts

Place all the cheeses in a bowl. Blend in the soup mix and beat thoroughly. Add the onions and Tabasco to taste.

Shape the mixture into a rectangular block. Wrap in cling film and chill in the refrigerator until firm.

Cut into 2.5 cm (1 inch) cubes. Chop the peanuts very finely, then toss the cheese cubes in them to coat. Arrange on a serving plate and chill until required.
Serves 8 to 10

Garlic Sausage Spears

80 g (2¾ oz)
  Boursin with
  garlic
75 g (3 oz) medium-
  fat curd cheese
salt
200 g (7 oz) garlic
  sausage, sliced
1/2 lettuce, shredded

Place the Boursin and curd cheese in a bowl and blend together, adding salt to taste.

Divide the mixture between the garlic sausage slices. Roll up and secure each with a cocktail stick.

Arrange the lettuce on a plate and place the spears on top.
Makes about 20

Sage and Onion Quiche

PASTRY:
*175 g (6 oz) plain
    flour*
pinch of salt
*40 g (1½ oz)
    margarine*
40 g (1½ oz) lard
*1½ tablespoons
    water*

FILLING:
15 g (½ oz) butter
1 onion, chopped
*50 g (2 oz) ham,
    chopped*
*50 g (2 oz) peas,
    cooked*
*75 g (3 oz) sage
    Derby cheese,
    grated*
2 eggs, beaten
150 ml (¼ pint) milk
*½ teaspoon dried
    sage*
salt and pepper

Sift the flour and salt into a bowl. Rub in the fats until the mixture resembles fine breadcrumbs. Add the water and mix to a firm dough. Knead lightly, then chill for 15 minutes.

Roll out and use to line a 20 cm (8 inch) flan dish or tin. Prick the base.

For the filling, melt the butter in a pan, add the onion and fry until soft. Spread the onion, ham, peas and 50 g (2 oz) of the cheese in the pastry case.

Combine the eggs, milk, sage, and salt and pepper to taste. Pour into the pastry case and sprinkle with the remaining cheese. Bake in a preheated moderately hot oven, 190°C (375°F), Gas Mark 5, for 40 to 45 minutes or until firm and golden. Serve hot or cold.

Serves 4

Country Vegetable Flan

PASTRY:
50 g (2 oz) wholemeal flour
125 g (4 oz) plain flour, sifted
pinch of salt
40 g (1½ oz) margarine
40 g (1½ oz) lard
1½ tablespoons water

FILLING:
1 large carrot
1 leek
salt and pepper
25 g (1 oz) butter
25 g (1 oz) plain flour
300 ml (½ pint) milk
125 g (4 oz) Farmhouse Cheddar cheese, grated
½ teaspoon made mustard
50 g (2 oz) each broad beans, peas and sweetcorn, cooked

Mix the flours and salt together in a bowl. Continue with the pastry as for Sage and Onion Quiche (see opposite). Roll out and use to line a 20 cm (8 inch) flan ring on a baking sheet. Bake blind in a preheated moderately hot oven, 190°C (375°F), Gas Mark 5, for 15 minutes. Remove the beans and foil and return to the oven for 5 minutes.

Meanwhile, make the filling. Slice the carrot and leek, then cook separately in boiling salted water until tender; drain. Melt the butter in a pan, stir in the flour and cook for 1 minute. Gradually blend in the milk, then heat, stirring, until thickened. Add 75 g (3 oz) cheese, the mustard, vegetables, and salt and pepper to taste.

Turn into the flan case and sprinkle with the remaining cheese. Place under a preheated moderate grill until the cheese is bubbling. Serve immediately.
Serves 4

Mediterranean Quiche

PASTRY:

*175 g (6 oz) plain
  flour*
pinch of salt
*40 g (1½ oz)
  margarine*
40 g (1½ oz) lard
*1½ tablespoons
  water*

FILLING:

*1 × 198 g (7 oz)
  can tuna fish*
1 onion, chopped
*1 clove garlic, crushed
  (optional)*
2 eggs, beaten
*113 g (4 oz) medium-
  fat curd cheese*
*150 ml (¼ pint)
  single cream*
*1 tablespoon chopped
  chives*
salt and pepper
*1 tablespoon grated
  Parmesan cheese*
*8 black olives,
  halved*

Sift the flour and salt into a bowl.
Rub in the fat until the mixture
resembles fine breadcrumbs. Add the
water and mix to a firm dough.
Knead lightly, then chill for 15
minutes.

Roll out and use to line a 20 cm
(8 inch) flan dish. Prick the base.

To make the filling, drain and
flake the tuna, reserving
1 tablespoon oil. Heat this oil in a
pan, add the onion and garlic and fry
until soft. Place in the pastry case
with the tuna.

Blend the eggs, curd cheese and
cream together. Stir in the chives,
and salt and pepper to taste. Pour
into the flan case, sprinkle with the
Parmesan cheese and arrange the
olive halves on top.

Bake in a preheated moderately
hot oven, 190°C (375°F), Gas Mark
5, for 40 to 45 minutes or until firm
and golden. Serve hot or cold.
Serves 4

Wholemeal Pizza

125 g (4 oz)
  self-raising flour
1 teaspoon baking
  powder
pinch of salt
125 g (4 oz)
  wholemeal flour
50 g (2 oz) margarine
150 ml (¼ pint) milk
TOPPING:
6 tablespoons tomato
  chutney
1 tablespoon oil
350 g (12 oz)
  onions, sliced
4 tomatoes, skinned
  and sliced
2 teaspoons chopped
  mixed herbs
75 g (3 oz) ham,
  chopped
75 g (3 oz) Cheddar
  cheese, grated
2 × 62.5 g (2.2 oz)
  packets soft cream
  cheese
salt and pepper

Sift the self-raising flour, baking powder and salt into a bowl. Stir in the wholemeal flour. Rub in the fat until the mixture resembles bread-crumbs. Stir in the milk and mix to a soft dough. Turn onto a floured surface and knead until smooth.

Roll out to a 28 cm (11 inch) circle. Pinch a slight rim around the edge. Place on an oiled baking sheet and spread with the chutney.

Heat the oil in a pan, add the onions and fry until soft. Remove from the pan with a slotted spoon and place on top of the chutney. Cover with the tomato slices and sprinkle with the herbs, ham and grated cheese. Cut the cream cheese into olive-size pieces and place on top of the filling. Season well with salt and pepper.

Bake in a preheated moderately hot oven, 200°C (400°F), Gas Mark 6, for 20 to 30 minutes or until the dough is cooked and the cheese is bubbling. Serve immediately.

Serves 4

Italian Pizzas

BASE:
½ × 567 g (20 oz)
  packet white bread
  mix
200 ml (⅓ pint)
  water
2 teaspoons oil
TOPPING:
2 × 397 g (14 oz)
  cans tomatoes,
  drained
2 teaspoons dried
  oregano
175 g (6 oz)
  Mozzarella or
  Gruyère cheese,
  sliced
salt and pepper
2 × 49 g (1¾ oz)
  cans anchovies,
  drained
24 black olives,
  halved
50 g (2 oz) Parmesan
  cheese, grated

Make up the bread mix with the water as directed on the packet. Turn onto a floured surface and knead for 2 minutes. Place in a bowl, cover and leave to rise in a warm place for 20 to 30 minutes, or until the dough has doubled in size.

Turn onto a floured surface and knead for 5 minutes. Divide into 4 pieces and roll out each to a 15 cm (6 inch) circle. Brush with a little oil and place on oiled baking sheets.

Arrange the tomatoes over the pizzas. Top with the oregano, Mozzarella or Gruyère, and salt and pepper to taste. Slice the anchovies lengthways and arrange in a lattice pattern over the cheese. Place the olives in the squares and sprinkle with the Parmesan cheese.

Bake in a preheated moderately hot oven, 200°C (400°F), Gas Mark 6, for 20 to 25 minutes until the cheese is bubbling. Serve immediately.
Makes 4

Garlic and Pepper Pizzas

4 pizza bases (see
  above)
2 × 397 g (14 oz)
  cans tomatoes,
  drained and
  chopped
1 tablespoon oil
1 onion, chopped
1 green pepper, cored,
  seeded and chopped
125 g (4 oz) Emmen-
  tal cheese, sliced
125 g (4 oz) garlic
  sausage, sliced
1 tablespoon chopped
  mixed herbs
50 g (2 oz) Parmesan
  cheese, grated

Place the prepared pizzas on oiled baking sheets and cover with the tomatoes.

Heat the oil in a pan, add the onion and green pepper and fry until soft. Spoon over the tomatoes. Cover with the sliced cheese then the garlic sausage. Sprinkle with the herbs and Parmesan cheese. Bake as for Italian Pizzas (above). Serve immediately.
Makes 4

Bacon and Mushroom Pizzas

4 pizza bases (see
    opposite)
2 × 397 g (14 oz)
    cans tomatoes
2 teaspoons grated
    onion
250 g (8 oz)
    matured Cheddar
    cheese, grated
6 rashers streaky
    bacon, derinded
50 g (2 oz)
    mushrooms, sliced
oil for brushing

Place the prepared pizza bases on
oiled baking sheets. Drain and chop
the tomatoes, then spread over the
bases.

   Sprinkle the onion and 175 g (6 oz)
of the cheese over the tomatoes.
Stretch the bacon and cut into strips.
Arrange in a lattice pattern over the
cheese and place the mushrooms in
the squares, brushing them with a
little oil. Sprinkle with the remaining
cheese. Bake as for Italian pizzas
(opposite). Serve immediately.
Makes 4

Nutty Chicken Bake

4 chicken portions,
  skinned
1 onion, sliced
50 g (2 oz) salted
  peanuts
1 × 298 g (10½ oz)
  can condensed
  celery soup
150 ml (¼ pint)
  milk
salt and pepper
50 g (2 oz) Leicester
  cheese, grated
25 g (1 oz) fresh
  breadcrumbs
parsley sprigs to
  garnish

Place the chicken portions, onion and half the peanuts in a 1.75 litre (3 pint) casserole. Mix the soup with the milk and add salt and pepper to taste. Pour over the chicken. Cover and cook in a preheated moderate oven, 180°C (350°F), Gas Mark 4, for 1¼ hours.

Crush the remaining peanuts and mix with the cheese and breadcrumbs. Remove the casserole lid and sprinkle the mixture over the chicken. Return to the oven, uncovered, for 20 minutes or until the topping is crisp and golden. Garnish with parsley and serve immediately.
Serves 4

Country Veal Casserole

2 tablespoons oil
600 g (1¼ lb) pie
  veal
1 onion, sliced
2 celery sticks,
  chopped
1 green pepper, cored,
  seeded and chopped
25 g (1 oz) plain
  flour
300 ml (½ pint)
  apple juice
300 ml (½ pint)
  light stock
50 g (2 oz) raisins
25 g (1 oz) walnuts,
  chopped
50 g (2 oz) dried
  apricots
salt and pepper
142 ml (5 fl oz)
  soured cream
50 g (2 oz) Cheshire
  cheese, grated

Cut the veal into 2.5 cm (1 inch) cubes. Heat the oil in a pan, add the veal and fry until evenly browned. Remove with a slotted spoon and place in a 2.25 litre (4 pint) casserole.

Add the onion, celery and green pepper to the pan and fry for 1 minute. Stir in the flour and cook for 1 minute. Gradually stir in the apple juice and stock. Heat, stirring, until the sauce thickens. Add the raisins, walnuts, apricots, and salt and pepper to taste. Cook for 2 minutes, then pour over the veal. Cover and cook in a preheated moderate oven, 160°C (325°F), Gas Mark 3, for 2 hours.

Check seasoning, then spoon the soured cream over the meat. Sprinkle with the cheese and return to the oven, uncovered, for 10 minutes.

Serve immediately, with rice.
Serves 4

Apple and Cheese Burgers

125 g (4 oz)
  matured Cheddar
  cheese, grated
3 dessert apples
few drops
  Worcestershire
  sauce
grated rind of
  ½ orange
4 baconburgers
parsley sprigs to
  garnish

Set aside 2 tablespoons cheese and put the rest in a bowl. Peel, core and grate 2 apples and add to the cheese with the Worcestershire sauce and orange rind. Mix well.

Cook the baconburgers under a preheated moderate grill for 15 minutes, turning once. Spread the cheese mixture over each burger. Core remaining apple and cut into 4 slices. Place one on each burger and sprinkle with remaining cheese. Return to the grill for 3 to 4 minutes. Garnish with parsley to serve.
Serves 4

Bacon, Cheese and Apple Plait

SHORTCRUST PASTRY:
250 g (8 oz) plain
  flour
pinch of salt
50 g (2 oz) margarine
50 g (2 oz) lard
2 tablespoons water
beaten egg to glaze
FILLING:
1 onion
1 cooking apple,
  peeled and cored
250 g (8 oz) lean
  bacon, derinded
1 large slice bread,
  crusts removed
50 g (2 oz) Cheddar
  cheese, grated
2 teaspoons ground
  coriander
½ teaspoon curry
  powder
1 teaspoon mixed
  herbs
pinch of dry mustard
salt and pepper
TO GARNISH:
shredded lettuce

Sift the flour and salt into a bowl. Rub in the fats until the mixture resembles fine breadcrumbs. Add the water and mix to a firm dough. Turn onto a floured surface and knead lightly. Chill for 15 minutes.

Meanwhile, make the filling. Mince the onion, apple, bacon and bread. Add the cheese, coriander, curry powder, herbs, mustard, and salt and pepper to taste. Mix well.

Roll out the pastry to a rectangle, 30 × 25 cm (12 × 10 inches), and trim the edges. Place the filling down the centre, then cut slanting strips 1 cm (½ inch) apart down each side of the pastry. Dampen the edges with water and plait the strips over the filling by taking them alternately from each side.

Brush the plait with beaten egg and bake in a preheated moderately hot oven, 190°C (375°F), Gas Mark 5, for 30 to 40 minutes, or until golden brown and crisp.

Serve hot or cold, garnished with lettuce.
Serves 4

Caerphilly-Topped Kidneys

25 g (1 oz) butter
1 onion, chopped
350 g (12 oz) lambs'
  kidneys, cored and
  chopped
1½ tablespoons flour
150 ml (¼ pint)
  stock
1 tablespoon sherry
125 g (4 oz) button
  mushrooms, sliced
salt and pepper
175 g (6 oz) brown
  rice, cooked

TOPPING:
2 eggs
150 ml (¼ pint) milk
75 g (3 oz) Caerphilly
  cheese, grated
½ teaspoon dried
  mixed herbs

Melt the butter in a pan, add the
onion and fry until soft. Add the
kidneys and cook gently for
5 minutes. Stir in the flour and cook
for 1 minute. Remove from the heat
and stir in the stock and sherry.
Heat, stirring, until the sauce
thickens. Add the mushrooms, and
salt and pepper to taste.

Transfer to a greased 1.75 litre (3
pint) ovenproof dish. Spoon the rice
over the kidneys and level the top.

Beat the eggs and milk together,
then add the cheese, herbs, and salt
and pepper to taste. Pour over the
rice and cook in a preheated
moderately hot oven, 190°C (375°F),
Gas Mark 5, for 20 to 30 minutes,
until set and golden. Serve
immediately.
Serves 4

Cheesy Beef Olives

6-8 slices beef
  topside, 5 mm
  (¼ inch) thick
2 tablespoons oil
1 onion, sliced
125 g (4 oz) button
  mushrooms
1 tablespoon flour
300 ml (½ pint)
  tomato juice
150 ml (¼ pint) beef
  stock
salt and pepper
1 bay leaf
STUFFING:
125 g (4 oz) fresh
  white breadcrumbs
50 g (2 oz) Cheddar
  cheese, grated
2 teaspoons each
  chopped chives and
  parsley
1 clove garlic, crushed
1 egg
TO GARNISH:
chopped parsley

Mix together all the stuffing ingredients, with salt and pepper to taste, and divide between the beef slices. Roll up and secure with string.

Heat the oil in a large pan and fry the onion until transparent. Transfer to a casserole, using a slotted spoon. Add the beef olives to the pan and brown lightly, then place in the casserole with the mushrooms.

Add the flour to the pan and cook, stirring, until it begins to brown. Gradually blend in the tomato juice and stock and heat, stirring, until the sauce thickens. Season with salt and pepper to taste.

Pour the sauce over the beef olives and add the bay leaf. Cover and cook in a preheated moderate oven, 180°C (350°F), Gas Mark 4, for 1½ hours.

Remove the olives, discard the string and place on a warmed serving dish. Spoon some sauce over and sprinkle with parsley. Serve the remaining sauce separately.
Serves 4 to 6

Velvet Carbonnade

750 g (1½ lb) lean
    stewing steak
50 g (2 oz) bacon
2 tablespoons oil
3 tablespoons flour
300 ml (½ pint)
    stout
300 ml (½ pint) beef
    stock
2 tablespoons vinegar
1 tablespoon brown
    sugar
2 cloves garlic, crushed
500 g (1 lb) onions,
    sliced
2 carrots, sliced
salt and pepper
1 bouquet garni
TOPPING:
4 thick slices buttered
    French bread
made mustard
75 g (3 oz) Cheddar
    cheese, grated

Cut the meat into 1 cm (½ inch) cubes. Derind and chop the bacon. Heat the oil in a flameproof casserole, add the meat and bacon, and fry until evenly browned. Remove with a slotted spoon and set aside.

Add the flour to the pan and cook, stirring, until lightly browned. Gradually stir in the stout, stock and vinegar. Heat, stirring, until the sauce thickens. Add the sugar.

Layer the garlic, onions, carrots and meat in the casserole, sprinkling with salt and pepper. Pour the sauce over, add the bouquet garni, cover and cook in a preheated cool oven, 150°C (300°F), Gas Mark 2, for 3 to 3½ hours.

Spread the bread with mustard. Remove the bouquet garni from the casserole and arrange the bread on top. Sprinkle with the cheese and place under a preheated moderate grill until the cheese is bubbling.

Serves 4

Gloucester Corn Pie

PASTRY:
250 g (8 oz) plain
  flour
pinch of salt
50 g (2 oz) margarine
50 g (2 oz) lard
2 tablespoons water
beaten egg to glaze

FILLING:
25 g (1 oz) butter
25 g (1 oz) flour
300 ml (½ pint) milk
75 g (3 oz) ham,
  chopped
½ × 340 g (12 oz) can
  sweetcorn, drained
125 g (4 oz) Double
  Gloucester cheese,
  grated
½ teaspoon made
  mustard
1 tablespoon chopped
  parsley
salt and pepper
1 hard-boiled egg

Make the pastry as for Bacon, Cheese and Apple Plait (see page 54) and chill for 30 minutes. Roll out two thirds of the pastry and use to line a 20 cm (8 inch) pie plate.

Melt the butter in a pan, stir in the flour and cook for 1 minute. Stir in the milk, then heat, stirring, until thickened. Add the other filling ingredients, except the egg. Place half the mixture in the pastry case. Slice the egg and arrange on top. Cover with the remaining filling.

Roll out the remaining pastry to make a lid. Dampen the edges and place the lid over the pie, sealing the edges well. Trim and flute the edges. Decorate with leaves made from pastry trimmings. Brush the pastry with beaten egg.

Bake in a preheated moderately hot oven, 200°C (400°F), Gas Mark 6, for 25 to 30 minutes or until golden brown. Serve hot or cold.
Serves 4

Tuna Gougère

CHOUX PASTRY:
150 ml (¼ pint)
  water
50 g (2 oz) butter
65 g (2½ oz) plain
  flour, sifted
salt and pepper
2 eggs, beaten
50 g (2 oz) Cheddar
  cheese, grated
FILLING:
15 g (½ oz) butter
1 onion chopped
1 tablespoon flour
150 ml (¼ pint) stock
150 ml (¼ pint) milk
2 tomatoes, skinned
  and chopped
1 × 198 g (7 oz)
  can tuna fish,
  drained and flaked
1 tablespoon grated
  Parmesan cheese
1 tablespoon fresh
  breadcrumbs
chopped parsley to
  garnish

Place the water and butter in a
saucepan and bring to the boil.
Remove from the heat and quickly
beat in all the flour, with a pinch
each of salt and pepper. Beat
vigorously until the mixture is
smooth and leaves the side of the
pan. Cool slightly, then beat in the
eggs, a little at a time. Stir in the
cheese. Spoon the mixture around
the sides of a greased 20 cm (8 inch)
flan dish or pie plate.

For the filling, melt the butter in a
pan, add the onion and fry until soft.
Stir in the flour and cook for
1 minute. Gradually stir in the stock
and milk, then heat, stirring, until
thickened. Add the tomatoes, tuna
and salt and pepper to taste. Spoon
into the choux ring.

Sprinkle the Parmesan and
breadcrumbs over the filling. Cook
in a preheated moderately hot oven,
200°C (400°F), Gas Mark 6, for 30 to
40 minutes, until risen and golden.

Garnish with parsley to serve.
Serves 4

Seafood Pancakes

PANCAKES:
125 g (4 oz) plain flour
pinch of salt
1 egg
300 ml (½ pint) milk
oil for frying

FILLING:
25 g (1 oz) butter
1 clove garlic, crushed
1 onion, finely chopped
25 g (1 oz) plain flour
300 ml (½ pint) milk
75 g (3 oz) Gruyère cheese, grated
salt and pepper
4 tablespoons single cream
125 g (4 oz) frozen peeled prawns, thawed
50 g (2 oz) mussels, cooked
2 scallops, cooked and sliced

TO GARNISH:
parsley sprigs
whole prawns (optional)

Sift the flour and salt into a bowl. Make a well in the centre and add the egg and half the milk. Beat until smooth, then stir in the remaining milk.

Lightly oil an 18 cm (7 inch) non–stick frying pan and place over a moderate heat. Pour in enough batter to cover the base. Cook until the underside is lightly browned, then turn and cook the other side. Repeat with the remaining batter to make 8 pancakes.

Stack the pancakes on a plate, with a piece of greaseproof paper between each one. Place over a pan of simmering water to keep hot while making the filling.

Melt the butter in a pan, add the garlic and onion and fry until soft. Stir in the flour and cook for 1 minute. Remove from the heat and gradually blend in the milk. Return to the heat, stirring, until the sauce thickens. Remove from the heat and stir in 50 g (2 oz) of the cheese, and salt and pepper to taste.

Place 4 tablespoons of the sauce in a bowl and stir in the cream; keep on one side. Add the prawns, mussels and scallops to the sauce in the pan and heat through gently. Divide the mixture between the pancakes and roll up. Arrange in a greased shallow heatproof dish. Pour the reserved sauce over the pancakes and sprinkle with the remaining cheese. Place under a preheated moderate grill for 5 minutes until the cheese is bubbling and golden.

Serve immediately, garnished with parsley sprigs and whole prawns, if using.
Serves 4

Savoury Topped Fish

4 cod steaks
2 tablespoons lemon juice
salt and pepper
25 g (1 oz) butter
1 onion, finely chopped
1 green pepper, cored, seeded and chopped
3 tomatoes, skinned and chopped
3 teaspoons chopped parsley
50 g (2 oz) fresh white breadcrumbs
75 g (3 oz) Cheddar cheese, grated

Place the fish in a greased, shallow, ovenproof dish. Spoon over the lemon juice and sprinkle with salt and pepper.

Melt the butter in a pan, add the onion and green pepper and fry until soft. Stir in the tomatoes, 2 teaspoons parsley, the breadcrumbs, cheese, and salt and pepper to taste.

Spoon the mixture over the fish. Cover tightly with foil and cook in a preheated moderate oven, 180°C (350°F), Gas Mark 4, for 30 minutes or until the fish is tender. Sprinkle with the remaining parsley to serve.
Serves 4

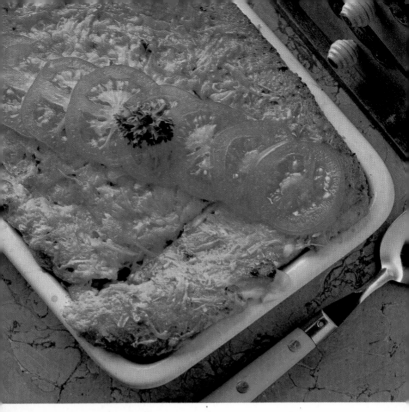

Wholemeal Cheese Pudding

8 slices buttered
   wholemeal bread
75 g (3 oz)
   Lancashire cheese,
   grated
75 g (3 oz) Leicester
   cheese, grated
3 eggs
450 ml (¾ pint)
   milk
1 teaspoon made
   mustard
1 teaspoon caraway
   seeds (optional)
1 tablespoon chopped
   parsley
salt and pepper
TO GARNISH:
tomato slices
parsley sprig

Make sandwiches with the bread and
Lancashire cheese. Remove the crusts
and cut into triangles. Arrange in a
shallow greased 1.2 litre (2 pint)
ovenproof dish. Sprinkle with 50 g
(2 oz) of the Leicester cheese.

Whisk together the eggs, milk,
mustard, caraway seeds if using,
parsley, and salt and pepper to taste.
Pour over the bread and leave to
stand for 30 minutes.

Sprinkle with the remaining cheese
and bake in a preheated moderate
oven, 160°C (325°F), Gas Mark 3, for
40 to 45 minutes, or until set and
golden. Serve immediately,
garnished with tomato and parsley.
Serves 4

Classic Cheese Soufflé

50 g (2 oz) butter
40 g (1½ oz) plain
   flour
300 ml (½ pint)
   milk
4 eggs, separated
75 g (3 oz) Gruyère
   cheese, grated
1 tablespoon grated
   Parmesan cheese
¼ teaspoon made
   mustard
salt and pepper

Melt the butter in a large pan. Stir in the flour and cook for 1 minute. Remove from the heat and gradually blend in the milk. Heat, stirring, until thickened. Beat in the egg yolks and cheeses. Season with the mustard, and salt and pepper to taste.

Whisk the egg whites until thick but not dry. Using a metal spoon, fold a quarter into the cheese mixture, then fold in the remainder.

Turn into an oiled 1.2 litre (2 pint) soufflé dish and bake in a preheated moderately hot oven, 190°C (375°F), Gas Mark 5, for 35 to 40 minutes until well risen and golden. Serve immediately.

Serves 4

VARIATIONS: Use only 50 g (2 oz) good flavoured hard cheese. Add 50 g (2 oz) of any one of the following to the basic sauce: chopped chicken or ham; peeled prawns; chopped mushrooms; flaked mackerel.

VEGETABLES & SALADS

The dishes in this section are sufficient to serve as a light meal with bread, rolls, pasta or rice. The exception is Green Salad with Roquefort Dressing, which is best served with cold meats or fish.

Camembert Leeks

750 g (1½ lb) leeks
salt and pepper
25 g (1 oz) butter
1 tablespoon finely
  chopped onion
25 g (1 oz) plain
  flour
300 ml (½ pint)
  milk
125 g (4 oz)
  Camembert
  cheese, derinded
  and chopped
1 hard-boiled egg,
  finely chopped
chopped parsley to
  garnish

Cut the leeks in half lengthways and wash thoroughly. Cook in boiling salted water for 8 minutes, or until tender. Drain and place in a shallow heatproof dish; keep warm.

Melt the butter in a pan, add the onion and fry until soft. Stir in the flour and cook for 1 minute. Gradually blend in the milk. Heat, stirring, until the sauce thickens. Add the cheese, egg, and salt and pepper to taste. Heat gently, then pour over the leeks.

Garnish with parsley and serve immediately.
Serves 4

Marrow, Onion and Tomato Gratin

1 medium marrow
15 g (½ oz) butter
1 large onion, sliced
1 clove garlic, crushed
1 × 397 g (14 oz) can tomatoes
1 teaspoon each dried basil and oregano
salt and pepper
75 g (3 oz) Cheddar cheese, grated
25 g (1 oz) Gruyère cheese, grated
75 g (3 oz) fresh breadcrumbs

Peel the marrow, halve lengthwise and remove the seeds. Cut the flesh into 2.5 cm (1 inch) pieces.

Melt the butter in a large pan, add the onion and garlic and fry until soft. Add the marrow, tomatoes with their juice, basil, oregano, and salt and pepper to taste. Bring to the boil, cover and simmer for 30 to 35 minutes or until the marrow is soft. Pour into a shallow, heatproof dish.

Mix together the cheeses and breadcrumbs. Sprinkle over the vegetables and place under a preheated moderate grill for 2 to 3 minutes until the topping is golden brown. Serve immediately.
Serves 4

Beany Cheese Crunch

75 g (3 oz) red
   kidney beans
75 g (3 oz) black eye
   beans
75 g (3 oz) butter
   beans
1 large onion
2 celery sticks
50 g (2 oz) bacon,
   derinded
2 tablespoons oil
1 clove garlic,
   crushed
1 × 397 g (14 oz)
   can tomatoes
150 ml (¼ pint)
   light stock
¼ teaspoon chilli
   powder
salt and pepper
75 g (3 oz)
   wholemeal
   breadcrumbs
125 g (4 oz)
   matured Cheddar
   cheese, grated

Soak the kidney, black eye and butter beans in cold water overnight. Drain and place in a saucepan. Cover with cold water, bring to the boil and boil rapidly for 10 minutes. Lower the heat, cover and simmer for 30 to 35 minutes or until tender. Drain and rinse under cold water.

Chop the onion, celery and bacon finely. Heat the oil in a pan, add the onion, garlic, celery and bacon and fry until soft. Add the tomatoes with their juice and the stock. Stir in the chilli powder, beans, and salt and pepper to taste. Bring to the boil, cover and simmer for 20 minutes. Transfer to a heatproof 1.2 litre (2 pint) dish.

Mix together the breadcrumbs and cheese and spoon over the bean mixture. Place under a preheated moderate grill until the topping is golden brown. Serve immediately.
Serves 4

Vegetable Hotpot

1 onion
250 g (8 oz) carrots
1 small cauliflower
4 tomatoes
1 tablespoon oil
300 ml (½ pint)
    light stock
1 tablespoon tomato
    purée
1 teaspoon dried
    mixed herbs
salt and pepper
125 g (4 oz) each
    frozen green beans
    and peas
50 g (2 oz) unsalted
    peanuts
DUMPLINGS:
50 g (2 oz)
    self-raising flour
25 g (1 oz) suet
½ teaspoon dried
    mixed herbs
75 g (3 oz) Cheddar
    cheese, grated

Slice the onion and carrots. Break the cauliflower into florets. Skin and chop the tomatoes.

Heat the oil in a large pan, add the onion and carrots and fry for 5 minutes. Add the tomatoes, stock, tomato purée, herbs, and salt and pepper to taste. Bring to the boil, cover and simmer for 15 minutes. Add the cauliflower, beans, peas and nuts and cook for 15 minutes.

Meanwhile, make the dumplings. Sift the flour into a bowl and add the suet, herbs, 25 g (1 oz) of the cheese, and salt and pepper to taste. Stir in 4 tablespoons water and mix to an elastic dough. Turn onto a floured surface and, with floured hands, shape into 8 balls.

Place the dumplings on top of the vegetables. Sprinkle with the remaining cheese, cover and simmer for 30 minutes.

Transfer to a warmed serving dish and serve immediately.

Serves 4

Dutch Cauliflower Cheese

1 medium cauliflower
salt and pepper
40 g (1½ oz) butter
1 small onion,
    chopped
40 g (1½ oz) plain
    flour
300 ml (½ pint)
    milk
175 g (6 oz)
    matured Gouda
    cheese, grated
½ teaspoon made
    mustard
½ teaspoon caraway
    seeds (optional)
4 rashers streaky
    bacon, derinded
    and cut in half
1 rye crispbread,
    crushed

Discard outer leaves and stalk from the cauliflower and cut into quarters. Cook in boiling salted water for 7 minutes, or until just tender. Drain, reserving 150 ml (¼ pint) of the liquid. Place the cauliflower in a shallow ovenproof dish.

Melt the butter in a pan, add the onion and fry until soft. Stir in the flour and cook for 1 minute. Remove from the heat and gradually blend in the milk and reserved liquid. Heat, stirring, until the sauce thickens. Add 150 g (5 oz) of the cheese, the mustard, caraway seeds if using, and salt and pepper to taste. Heat through and pour over the cauliflower.

Stretch the bacon pieces and roll up. Cook under a preheated moderate grill until crisp.

Mix together the crispbread and remaining cheese. Sprinkle over the cauliflower and place under the grill until bubbling and golden brown. Garnish with the bacon rolls to serve.
Serves 4

Spinach Cannelloni

500 g (1 lb) frozen
chopped spinach,
thawed
175 g (6 oz)
matured Cheddar
cheese, grated
50 g (2 oz) fresh
breadcrumbs
salt and pepper
grated nutmeg
8 sheets of lasagne
25 g (1 oz) butter
25 g (1 oz) plain
flour
300 ml (½ pint)
milk
1 teaspoon made
mustard

Drain the spinach thoroughly and mix with 50 g (2 oz) of the cheese 40 g (1½ oz) of the breadcrumbs, and salt, pepper and nutmeg to taste.

Cook the lasagne in plenty of boiling salted water for 15 minutes or until just tender. Drain and rinse with cold water. Cut each piece in half and lay on a clean tea-towel. Divide the spinach mixture between the lasagne and roll up. Place in a greased shallow ovenproof dish.

Melt the butter in a pan, stir in the flour and cook for 1 minute. Slowly blend in the milk, then heat, stirring, until the sauce thickens. Add 75 g (3 oz) of the cheese, the mustard, and salt and pepper to taste. Pour over the cannelloni. Mix the remaining breadcrumbs and cheese, and sprinkle over the sauce.

Bake in a moderately hot oven, 190°C (375°F), Gas Mark 5, for 20 to 30 minutes or until the topping is golden.
Serves 4

Crispy Bacon Salad

125 g (4 oz) smoked
  bacon, derinded
2 hard-boiled eggs,
  chopped
175 g (6 oz) red
  Cheshire cheese,
  grated
50 g (2 oz) salted
  peanuts, chopped
3 tablespoons salad
  cream
1 tablespoon single
  cream
salt and pepper
1 lettuce
1 × 283 g (10 oz)
  can new potatoes
2 tomatoes, sliced
parsley sprigs to
  garnish

Cook the bacon under a preheated moderate grill until crisp and browned. Leave to cool, then chop and place in a bowl. Add the eggs, cheese, peanuts, salad cream and cream. Mix well together, adding salt and pepper to taste.

Arrange the lettuce leaves around the edge of a serving plate. Pile the bacon and cheese mixture in the centre.

Drain the potatoes and slice into rounds. Arrange the potatoes and tomatoes around the bacon salad and garnish with parsley.

Serves 4

Cheesy Chicken Salad

250 g (8 oz) cooked
  chicken
75 g (3 oz)
  Caerphilly cheese
250 g (8 oz) bean
  sprouts
1 green pepper, cored,
  seeded and sliced
1 tablespoon finely
  chopped onion
5 cm (2 inch) piece
  of cucumber, cut
  into strips
DRESSING:
4 tablespoons natural
  low-fat yogurt
4 tablespoons
  mayonnaise
1 clove garlic, crushed
1 teaspoon ground
  coriander
1 tablespoon soy sauce
salt and pepper

Cut the chicken into 2.5 cm (1 inch) pieces and the cheese into thin strips.

Mix together the bean sprouts, green pepper, onion, cucumber, chicken and cheese in a large bowl.

Mix the dressing ingredients together in another bowl, seasoning to taste with salt and pepper. Add to the salad, toss well together and transfer to a serving bowl.

Serves 4

Green Salad with Roquefort Dressing

1 small cos lettuce
½ cucumber, sliced
2 celery sticks,
    chopped
1 head of chicory,
    sliced
DRESSING:
75 g (3 oz) Roquefort
    cheese, crumbled
2 tablespoons milk
142 ml (5 fl oz)
    soured cream
salt and pepper

Tear the lettuce into pieces and place in a salad bowl. Add the cucumber, celery and chicory. Toss well together.

To make the dressing, place the cheese in a bowl and add the milk. Mash until smooth, then blend in the cream, and salt and pepper to taste. Pour over the salad just before serving.

Serves 4

71

Bavarian Salad

250 g (8 oz) white
cabbage, shredded
2 carrots, grated
1 celery stick,
chopped
1 head of chicory,
sliced
75 g (3 oz) smoked
Bavarian cheese,
cubed
75 g (3 oz)
Bavarian ham
sausage, skinned
and cubed
DRESSING:
3 tablespoons
mayonnaise
3 tablespoons natural
low-fat yogurt
1/2 teaspoon caraway
seeds, crushed
salt and pepper

Place the cabbage, carrots, celery,
chicory, cheese and ham sausage in a
bowl.

Mix together the dressing
ingredients, with salt and pepper to
taste, and add to the salad. Mix well
together and transfer to a serving
dish.

Serve with wholemeal or rye
bread.

Serves 4

Cheddar Egg Log with Salad

4 hard-boiled eggs,
chopped
250 g (8 oz)
matured Cheddar
cheese, grated
1 clove garlic, crushed
2 tablespoons
mayonnaise
2 tablespoons single
cream
1 tablespoon chopped
parsley
salt and pepper
SALAD:
1 lettuce
1/2 cucumber, sliced
1/2 green pepper,
cored, seeded and
sliced
4 tomatoes, sliced

Place the eggs, cheese, garlic,
mayonnaise, cream and chopped
parsley in a bowl. Mix well and add
salt and pepper to taste.

With wet hands, shape the mixture
into a roll. Wrap in foil and chill in
the refrigerator for at least 1 hour.

Arrange the salad ingredients at
the ends of an oval serving plate.
Slice the log into 8 pieces and arrange
along the middle of the plate. Serve
with rolls and butter.

Serves 4

Chick Pea and Havarti Mix

250 g (8 oz) chick
    peas
1 onion, finely
    chopped
2 cloves garlic, crushed
1 red pepper, cored,
    seeded and sliced
1 green pepper, cored,
    seeded and sliced
2 tablespoons chopped
    mixed herbs (e.g.
    parsley, chives,
    fennel, marjoram)
175 g (6 oz) Danish
    Havarti cheese,
    cubed

DRESSING:
½ teaspoon mustard
½ teaspoon sugar
1 tablespoon wine
    vinegar
4 tablespoons oil
salt and pepper

TO GARNISH:
chopped parsley

Soak the chick peas in cold water overnight, drain and place in a saucepan. Cover with cold water and bring to the boil. Boil for 10 minutes, then lower the heat, cover and simmer for 1 hour or until soft. Drain and rinse with cold water.

Place in a bowl with the onion, garlic, peppers, herbs and cheese.

To make the dressing, blend the mustard and sugar with the vinegar, then beat in the oil. Add salt and pepper to taste. Pour the dressing over the salad. Mix thoroughly and turn into a serving bowl. Sprinkle with parsley to serve.

Serves 4

Wensleydale Fruit Salad

2 red dessert apples
lemon juice
½ honeydew melon
1 × 227 g (8 oz)
    can pineapple
    slices, drained and
    chopped
50 g (2 oz) dates,
    stoned and chopped
2 tablespoons diced
    cucumber
2 celery sticks,
    chopped
175 g (6 oz)
    Wensleydale
    cheese, cubed
150 g (5 oz) natural
    low-fat yogurt
1 teaspoon sugar
    (optional)
lettuce to serve

Core and slice the apples and toss in lemon juice to prevent discoloration. Remove the skin from the melon and discard the seeds. Scoop the flesh into balls, using a melon baller, or cut into dice.

Mix together the apple, melon, pineapple, dates, cucumber, celery and cheese in a bowl. Stir in the yogurt and sugar, if using. Toss together well.

Pile the salad into a serving bowl lined with lettuce leaves. Serve immediately.
Serves 4

CHEESECAKES & OTHER DESSERTS

Cheesecakes can be served as a dessert, at teatime, or with coffee at any time. Most varieties freeze well for up to 2 months. Thaw in the refrigerator overnight, applying the fruit toppings and decorations just before serving, for best results.

Quick Orange Cheesecake

50 g (2 oz) butter
125 g (4 oz) digestive biscuits, crushed
227 g (8 oz) medium-fat curd cheese
150 g (5 oz) natural low-fat yogurt
½ packet orange jelly
3 tablespoons water
1 tablespoon sugar
grated rind and juice of 1 orange
1 × 212 g (7½ oz) can mandarin oranges, drained

Melt the butter in a pan. Remove from the heat and mix in the biscuit crumbs. Press into an oiled 20 cm (8 inch) flan ring placed on a serving plate. Chill in the refrigerator to harden.

Blend together the curd cheese and yogurt. Dissolve the jelly in the water over a low heat. Cool slightly, then stir in the sugar, orange rind and juice. Add to the cheese and whisk until smooth. Pour into the flan ring and leave in the refrigerator until set.

Carefully remove the flan ring and decorate the cheesecake with mandarin oranges. Serve chilled.
Serves 4 to 6

Chilled Raspberry Cheesecake

50 g (2 oz) butter
125 g (4 oz)
  digestive biscuits,
  crushed
227 g (8 oz) medium-
  fat curd cheese
113 g (4 oz) cottage
  cheese, sieved
75 g (3 oz) caster
  sugar
finely grated rind and
  juice of 1 lemon
15 g (½ oz) gelatine
2 tablespoons water
300 ml (½ pint)
  double cream,
  whipped
3 egg whites
175 g (6 oz)
  raspberries

Melt the butter in a pan. Remove from the heat and mix in the biscuit crumbs. Press into the base of an oiled 20 cm (8 inch) loose-bottomed cake tin. Chill in the refrigerator to harden.

Place the cheeses in a bowl and blend in the sugar, lemon rind and juice. Soak the gelatine in the water, then place the bowl over a pan of gently simmering water and stir until the gelatine has dissolved. Cool slightly, then stir into the cheese mixture. Fold in half of the cream.

Whisk the egg whites until stiff and fold in. Pour the filling over the biscuit base. Chill in the refrigerator until firm.

Carefully remove the cheesecake from the tin and place on a serving plate. Decorate with the remaining whipped cream and the raspberries.

Serves 8

NOTE: If fresh raspberries are not available, use frozen ones or a can of raspberry pie filling for the topping.

Blackcurrant Cheesecake

40 g (1½ oz) butter
75 g (3 oz) digestive
   biscuits, crushed
113 g (4 oz) medium-
   fat curd cheese
50 g (2 oz) cottage
   cheese, sieved
5 tablespoons
   blackcurrant
   yogurt
2 eggs, separated
1 tablespoon cornflour
finely grated rind of
   ½ lemon
40 g (1½ oz) caster
   sugar
TOPPING:
142 ml (5 fl oz)
   soured cream
½ × 397 g (14 oz)
   can blackcurrant
   pie filling
whipped cream
   (optional)

Melt the butter in a pan and stir in the biscuit crumbs. Press into the base of an oiled 18-20 cm (7-8 inch) loose-bottomed cake tin. Chill in the refrigerator to harden.

Place the cheeses in a bowl and blend in the yogurt, egg yolks, cornflour and lemon rind. Whisk the egg whites until stiff, fold in the sugar, then fold into the cheese mixture. Spoon over the biscuit base and bake in a preheated moderate oven, 180°C (350°F), Gas Mark 4, for 35 to 45 minutes or until firm.

Remove the cheesecake from the oven and spread the soured cream over the top. Return to the oven for 5 minutes. Cool in the tin.

Carefully remove the cheesecake from the tin and place on a serving plate. Spread the blackcurrant pie filling over the top and decorate with cream if wished. Serve chilled.

Serves 4 to 6

Chocolate Mint Cheesecake

50 g (2 oz) butter
125 g (4 oz)
    chocolate digestive
    biscuits, crushed
125 g (4 oz) plain
    chocolate, melted
4 tablespoons milk
2 × 62.5 g (2.2 oz)
    packets soft cream
    cheese
113 g (4 oz) cottage
    cheese, sieved
50 g (2 oz) caster
    sugar
½ teaspoon
    peppermint essence
½ teaspoon vanilla
    essence
15 g (½ oz) gelatine
300 ml (½ pint)
    double cream,
    whipped
chocolate mints to
    decorate

Melt the butter in a pan. Remove from the heat and stir in the biscuit crumbs. Mix well and press into the base of an oiled 18-20 cm (7-8 inch) loose-bottomed cake tin. Chill in the refrigerator to harden.

Melt the chocolate with the milk in a bowl over a pan of hot water. Place the cheeses in a bowl and blend in the sugar, essences and chocolate. Soak the gelatine in 4 tablespoons water, then place the bowl over a pan of simmering water to dissolve. Cool slightly and stir into the chocolate mixture.

Fold half of the cream into the filling. Spoon over the biscuit base and chill in the refrigerator until firm.

Carefully remove the cheesecake from the tin and place on a serving plate. Decorate with the reserved cream and chocolate mints.

Serves 6 to 8

Royal Curd Tart

250 g (8 oz) quantity
  shortcrust pastry
  (see page 54)
227 g (8 oz) medium-
  fat curd cheese
50 g (2 oz) ground
  almonds
50 g (2 oz) caster
  sugar
2 eggs, separated
grated rind and juice
  of 1 lemon
50 g (2 oz) sultanas
150 ml (¼ pint)
  double cream
sifted icing sugar to
  decorate

Roll out the pastry and use to line a
23 cm (9 inch) flan ring placed on a
baking sheet. Prick the base.

Place the cheese in a bowl and
blend in the ground almonds, caster
sugar and egg yolks. Add the lemon
rind and juice, sultanas and cream
and mix well. Whisk the egg whites
until stiff and fold into the mixture.
Pour into the flan case and bake in a
preheated moderately hot oven,
200°C (400°F), Gas Mark 6, for
20 minutes. Lower the temperature
to 180°C (350°F), Gas Mark 4, and
continue to cook for 30 to 35
minutes until firm and golden.

Serve warm or chilled, dusted
with icing sugar.

Serves 6

Ginger Cheesecake

75 g (3 oz) butter
175 g (6 oz)
   digestive biscuits,
   crushed
1 tablespoon ground
   ginger

FILLING:
227 g (8 oz) medium-
   fat curd cheese
2 tablespoons natural
   low-fat yogurt
2 eggs, separated
2 tablespoons soft
   brown sugar
2 pieces stem ginger,
   finely chopped
1 tablespoon ginger
   syrup (from jar)
grated nutmeg

TO DECORATE:
150 ml (¼ pint)
   double cream
stem ginger slices

Melt the butter in a pan. Remove from the heat and mix in the biscuit crumbs and ginger. Press into the base and sides of a 20 cm (8 inch) flan dish.

To make the filling, place the cheese in a bowl and blend in the yogurt, egg yolks and sugar. Stir in the ginger and syrup. Whisk the egg whites until stiff and fold into the cheese mixture. Pour into the flan case and sprinkle with grated nutmeg.

Bake in a preheated moderate oven, 160°C (325°F), Gas Mark 3, for 25 to 35 minutes until firm and golden. Allow to cool, then chill.

Whip the cream until thick. Decorate the cheesecake with piped whipped cream and ginger slices before serving.
Serves 6

Ginger and Marmalade Dreams

113 g (4 oz) medium-fat curd cheese
½ teaspoon ground ginger
2 tablespoons coarse-cut marmalade
2 tablespoons orange juice
1 tablespoon brandy
150 ml (¼ pint) double cream
few slices stem ginger to decorate

Place the cheese in a bowl and blend in the ginger, marmalade, orange juice and brandy. Whip the cream until it just holds its shape, then gently fold into the cheese mixture.

Spoon into 4 glass dishes and decorate with ginger. Chill before serving, with brandy snaps if liked.

Serves 4

Peach Fruit Layer

175 g (6 oz) medium-fat curd cheese
300 g (10 oz) peach melba yogurt
3 peaches, stoned and sliced
1 tablespoon sherry
25 g (1 oz) walnuts, chopped (optional)

Place the cheese in a bowl and blend in the yogurt. Set aside a few peach slices for decoration; mix the remainder with the sherry.

Spoon half the yogurt mixture into 4 tall glasses. Top with the peaches, then cover with the remaining yogurt mixture. Decorate with the reserved peach slices and walnuts, if using. Serve chilled.

Serves 4

Pineapple Crunch

113 g (4 oz) cottage cheese with pineapple
1 × 227 g (8 oz) can pineapple slices, drained
150 ml (¼ pint) double cream, whipped
25 g (1 oz) caster sugar
3 digestive sweetmeal biscuits, crushed
1 tablespoon sesame seeds, toasted

Place the cottage cheese in a bowl. Chop the pineapple finely and add to the cheese.

Place a third of the cream in a piping bag fitted with a star nozzle. Fold the remainder into the pineapple mixture with the sugar. Spoon into 4 individual dishes.

Mix together the biscuit crumbs and sesame seeds and sprinkle most of them over the desserts. Pipe a whirl of cream on each and sprinkle with the remaining crumbs. Serve chilled.

Serves 4

Mocha Dessert

1 tablespoon custard
  powder
1 teaspoon coffee
  granules
1 teaspoon cocoa
  powder
1½ tablespoons soft
  brown sugar
300 ml (½ pint)
  milk
½ teaspoon vanilla
  essence
113 g (4 oz) medium-
  fat curd cheese
2 dessert pears, peeled,
  halved and cored
grated nutmeg
chopped walnuts to
  decorate

Blend the custard powder, coffee, cocoa and sugar with a little of the milk. Heat the remaining milk until almost boiling, then pour onto the custard mixture, stirring. Return to the heat, stirring, until the custard thickens. Cool slightly and stir in the vanilla essence.

Place the cheese in a bowl and soften with a wooden spoon. Gradually blend in the custard, whisking if necessary, until smooth.

Place the pears in a serving dish and spoon the mocha mixture over. Sprinkle with grated nutmeg and decorate with walnuts. Serve chilled.
Serves 4

Lemon Cheese Meringue

25 g (1 oz) cornflour
300 ml (½ pint)
  milk
25 g (1 oz)
  granulated sugar
75 g (3 oz) medium-
  fat curd cheese
grated rind and juice
  of 1 lemon
2 eggs, separated
50 g (2 oz) caster
  sugar

Blend the cornflour with a little of the milk, then stir in the granulated sugar. Heat the remaining milk until almost boiling, then pour onto the blended custard, stirring. Return to the heat, stirring, until the custard thickens. Cool slightly.

Blend in the cheese, lemon rind and juice, and egg yolks. Whisk until smooth, then spoon into a greased 600 ml (1 pint) ovenproof dish.

Whisk the egg whites until stiff. Whisk in 25 g (1 oz) of the caster sugar, then fold in the remainder. Pile on top of the lemon custard and bake in a preheated moderately hot oven, 200°C (400°F), Gas Mark 6, for 15 minutes. Serve with cream.
Serves 4

Orange and Lemon Creams

2 × 62.5 g (2.2 oz)
 packets soft cream
 cheese
2 tablespoons natural
 low-fat yogurt
grated rind of
 ½ orange
grated rind and juice
 of ½ lemon
1 tablespoon caster
 sugar
2 small oranges
120 ml (4 fl oz)
 soured cream
25 g (1 oz) brown
 sugar
25 g (1 oz) flaked
 almonds
sponge fingers to
 serve

Place the cheese in a bowl and soften with a wooden spoon. Blend in the yogurt, orange rind, lemon rind and juice, and caster sugar. Place in 4 heatproof ramekin dishes.

Peel the oranges and divide into segments, removing all pith. Arrange the orange pieces on top of the cheese mixture.

Stir the soured cream until smooth and spoon over the oranges. Sprinkle with the brown sugar and almonds. Chill in the refrigerator until required.

Place under a preheated moderate grill for 3 to 4 minutes until the sugar melts and the nuts turn brown. Serve immediately, with sponge fingers.

Serves 4

Pancake Gâteau

PANCAKES:
125 g (4 oz) plain
 flour
pinch of salt
1 egg
300 ml (½ pint) milk
oil for frying
FILLING AND TOPPING:
4 bananas
113 g (4 oz) medium-
 fat curd cheese
1 teaspoon ground
 cinnamon
25 g (1 oz) soft
 brown sugar
2 tablespoons natural
 low-fat yogurt
250 g (8 oz)
 strawberries
1 tablespoon sherry
25 g (1 oz) caster
 sugar
juice of ½ lemon

Make and cook the pancakes as for Seafood Pancakes (see page 60). Keep warm while making the filling.

Mash 3 of the bananas with the cheese, cinnamon and sugar. Stir in the yogurt. Use the mixture to sandwich together the pancakes, stacking them one on top of the other on a warmed serving dish.

To make the sauce, sieve the strawberries or work in an electric blender until smooth. Stir in the sherry and sugar. Pour over the pancakes.

Slice the remaining banana and sprinkle with lemon juice. Arrange on top of the gâteau. Serve immediately, with cream.

Serves 4

NOTE: Fresh or frozen strawberries may be used for the topping.

BISCUITS, TEABREADS & CAKES

Baking is always satisfying, whether making a few scones or a complicated gâteau! The scone ring, teabread, and streusel cake are ideal for packed lunches, picnics, tea or supper snacks. The lemon dream sponge can be served as a dessert or for tea. All of these recipes freeze well.

Cheese and Peanut Biscuits

50 g (2 oz) self-raising flour
½ teaspoon baking powder
¼ teaspoon salt
50 g (2 oz) wholemeal flour
25 g (1 oz) margarine
25 g (1 oz) crunchy peanut butter
75 g (3 oz) Cheddar cheese, grated
25 g (1 oz) salted peanuts, finely chopped
1 large egg, beaten

Sift the self-raising flour, baking powder and salt into a bowl. Stir in the wholemeal flour. Rub in the margarine and peanut butter until the mixture resembles fine breadcrumbs. Stir in the cheese and peanuts. Bind the mixture together with the egg.

Turn onto a lightly floured surface and knead until smooth. Roll out to a 5 mm (¼ inch) thickness and cut out rounds, using a 5 cm (2 inch) biscuit cutter. Place, well apart on greased baking sheets.

Bake in a preheated moderately hot oven, 190°C (375°F), Gas Mark 5, for 10 to 15 minutes until lightly browned. Cool on a wire rack.

Makes about 25

Cottage Cheese and Date Teabread

250 g (8 oz)
    self-raising flour
pinch of salt
½ teaspoon mixed
    spice
25 g (1 oz) sugar
50 g (2 oz) butter
2 eggs
113 g (4 oz) cottage
    cheese
4 tablespoons milk
25 g (1 oz) walnuts,
    chopped
50 g (2 oz) sultanas

Sift the flour, salt and mixed spice into a bowl. Stir in the sugar and rub in the butter until the mixture resembles breadcrumbs.

Beat the eggs with the cheese and milk, then add to the dry ingredients, with the walnuts and sultanas. Mix well and spoon into a greased 500 g (1 lb) loaf tin. Bake in a preheated moderate oven, 180°C (350°F), Gas Mark 4, for 45 minutes, or until well risen and golden brown. Leave in the tin for 5 minutes, then turn onto a wire rack to cool.

Serve sliced and buttered.
Makes one 500 g (1 lb) loaf

Cheese and Bacon Loaf

75 g (3 oz) streaky
  bacon, derinded
  and chopped
1 small onion, finely
  chopped
250 g (8 oz)
  self-raising flour
1 teaspoon salt
pinch of pepper
50 g (2 oz)
  margarine
125 g (4 oz)
  matured Cheddar
  cheese, grated
2 eggs
150 ml (¼ pint)
  milk
1 teaspoon made
  mustard
1 tablespoon chopped
  parsley

Place the bacon in a non–stick pan and heat gently until the fat runs. Add the onion and cook for 5 to 7 minutes until soft. Drain on kitchen paper and leave to cool.

Sift the flour, salt and pepper into a bowl. Rub in the margarine until the mixture resembles breadcrumbs. Stir in the cheese, bacon and onion.

Beat the eggs with the milk, mustard and parsley. Add to the dry ingredients and beat thoroughly.

Turn into a greased 500 g (1 lb) loaf tin and bake in a preheated moderately hot oven, 190°C (375°F), Gas Mark 5, for 45 to 55 minutes, or until firm and golden. Leave in the tin for 5 minutes, then cool on a wire rack.

Serve sliced and buttered.
Makes one 500 g (1 lb) loaf

Cotswold Scone Ring

250 g (8 oz)
  self-raising flour
1 teaspoon baking
  powder
1 teaspoon salt
1 teaspoon dry
  mustard
40 g (1½ oz)
  margarine
125 g (4 oz) Cotswold
  with chives cheese,
  grated
150 ml (¼ pint) milk
beaten egg to glaze
TO SERVE:
2 × 62.5 g (2.2 oz)
  packets soft cream
  cheese
2 tablespoons
  chopped chives
½ teaspoon garlic
  granules

Sift the flour, baking powder, salt and mustard into a bowl. Rub in the margarine until the mixture resembles breadcrumbs. Stir in the cheese and milk and mix to a soft dough.

Turn onto a floured surface and knead until smooth. Roll out to 1 cm (½ inch) thickness. Using a 7.5 cm (3 inch) plain cutter, cut 8 scones. Arrange them in a circle, overlapping slightly, on a greased baking sheet. Brush with beaten egg and bake in a preheated hot oven, 220°C (425°F), Gas Mark 7, for 15 to 20 minutes, or until firm and golden brown. Turn onto a wire rack to cool slightly.

Mix together the cream cheese, chives and garlic granules. Break the scones apart while still warm, split each one and spread with the cheese mixture. Serve immediately.
Makes 8 scones

Cinnamon Streusel Cake

250 g (8 oz)
  self-raising flour
pinch of salt
1 teaspoon baking
  powder
125 g (4 oz) caster
  sugar
75 g (3 oz)
  margarine
2 eggs
113 g (4 oz) cottage
  cheese, sieved
150 ml (¼ pint)
  milk
1 tablespoon apricot
  jam, sieved
TOPPING:
50 g (2 oz) plain
  flour
50 g (2 oz) soft
  brown sugar
1½ teaspoons ground
  cinnamon
25 g (1 oz) butter,
  melted

Sift the flour, salt and baking powder into a bowl. Stir in the sugar and rub in the margarine until the mixture resembles breadcrumbs.

Beat the eggs with the cottage cheese, milk and jam. Add to the dry ingredients and beat to make a smooth batter. Spoon into a lined and greased 20 cm (8 inch) loose-bottomed cake tin.

To make the topping, stir the flour, sugar and cinnamon into the melted butter. Mix well and spoon over the cake mixture.

Bake in a preheated moderately hot oven, 190°C (375°F), Gas Mark 5, for 1 hour to 1 hour 10 minutes, or until rich brown in colour and firm to touch. Leave in the tin for 5 minutes, then turn onto a wire rack to cool.

Serve fresh as a cake or, when a few days old, sliced and spread with butter or cream cheese.

Makes one 20 cm (8 inch) cake

Lemon Dream Sponge

3 eggs
75 g (3 oz) caster
    sugar
75 g (3 oz) plain
    flour, sifted
finely grated rind and
    juice of ½ lemon
1 tablespoon sherry
FILLING:
75 g (3 oz) cream
    cheese
25 g (1 oz) icing
    sugar, sifted
finely grated rind of
    ½ lemon
2 teaspoons lemon
    juice
150 ml (¼ pint)
    double cream,
    whipped
TO DECORATE:
grated chocolate

Put the eggs and sugar in a bowl over a pan of hot water and whisk until the mixture is pale and thick enough to leave a trail. Remove the bowl from the pan and continue whisking until the mixture is cool.

Quickly fold in the flour and lemon rind. Divide between two lined and greased 18 cm (7 inch) sandwich tins. Bake in a preheated moderately hot oven, 190°C (375°F), Gas Mark 5, for 15 to 20 minutes, until firm and golden. Leave in the tins for 5 minutes then cool on a wire rack. Prick with a fork.

For the filling, soften the cheese in a bowl with a wooden spoon. Blend in the icing sugar, lemon rind and juice, then fold in the cream. Chill in the refrigerator for 1 hour.

Mix together the lemon juice and sherry and spoon over the cakes. Sandwich together with half the lemon cream; spread the remainder over the top. Decorate with grated chocolate and chill before serving.
Serves 6 to 8

INDEX